THE COMPLETE
SIBERIAN HUSKY

RINGPRESS

ACKNOWLEDGEMENTS

We have attempted to provide you with a flavour of all aspects of this most wonderful working breed. In addition, considerable research has been undertaken in providing the background to the Siberian Husky in a number of countries. For this we owe our heartfelt thanks to many friends for their help and photographs, including: Pam Thomas, Kim Leblanc, Nancy Van Gelderen-Parker, Michelle Menger, Olli Kaarnisto, Anneliese Braun-Witschel, Philippe Bescond, Dorle Linzenmeier, Daniela Vidal Leaver, Rikki Bergendahl, Angelo Bernardini, Barbara Fisk, Elsie Chadwick, Maya Brunner, Elly and Jorgen Hansen, Rosemary and Don Hooker, Leigh and Susan Gilchrist, Tom and Annette Iliffe, Kathy Stewart, Brent and Kathy Thomas, Sandy Cairns, Anna-Lee Forsberg, Julie McGuire, Richard Smith, Annie Jackson, Thierry Fontaine, Val Stockman.

Published by Ringpress Books Ltd,
PO Box 8, Lydney, Gloucestershire GL15 4YN

Designed by Sara Howell & Rob Benson

First Published 2002
© 2002 RINGPRESS BOOKS

ISBN 1 86054 290 5

Printed and bound in Singapore
by Kyodo Printing Co

10 9 8 7 6 5 4 3 2 1

FOREWORD

The stunning coat and classic outline of the Siberian Husky paint a picture in the minds of us all. It is of the relationship between man and dog against a background of mutual dependence. It is the wilderness, with a team of dogs straining in their harness to work for their master and friend. It is dogs, the wind, the snow and excitement. People have tried to live that life by owning one of these charismatic creatures.

No one really knows why the wolf, the Husky's ancestor, who was a lone and timid pack animal, befriended man, but it was a marriage made in heaven. These were two beings who could share communal facilities and fulfil a mutual need. Perhaps the dog worked harder at the relationship and finally came to be regarded as a working companion.

Work, in the case of the early Siberian Husky, was probably as a pack animal and hunting companion. The Siberian's size would lead us to believe that freight sled pulling was not what it was originally developed for. The companionable manner of the Siberian Husky would also lead us to believe that this was a dog living with man as an equal, in a struggle to survive against the most harsh of seasonal conditions.

Yet in the midst of this cosy continuity, human history was unfolding on another continent – historical events which would eventually bring this dog of superb temperament and beauty into the forefront of the world of working dogs.

It was the Alaskan Gold Rush – the discovery and development of an unknown territory. Alaska was a harsh, magnificent land that allowed the sled dog to fulfil what seems, with hindsight, its true reason for being. It was the means by which man could discover, trade and prosper in this unforgiving wilderness. The dog team allowed life to exist and progress with the speed that man craved.

But man is ingenious and at all levels the demand for new challenges exists. The natural excitement of competition for pleasure between men was nothing new, and so the sled dog race was born. This was the pride of working with a team of dogs that could perform better than those of your friends and competitors.

Then an Alaskan fur trader, named Goosak, came across the small, light Huskies of Siberia, and he had found a dog strong enough and willing to pull a sled, yet relatively small, well built and able to perform this task at speed. The Siberian Husky had arrived.

Its impact was instant: a new perspective was presented to sled dog drivers. This working dog made another impact in the dog world. Its stunning good looks, majestic lines and classic markings cast their spell on all who happened upon them. This beauty was further developed and sought after for both the show ring and as a proud pet owner's prized possession. Yet one constant factor has never left this dog – its sled dog heritage. This has been paramount in retaining the Siberian Husky's abilities. Most owners of this unique sled dog either participate in some form of the sport at one level or other, or else longingly dream of it.

The Siberian Husky has never forgotten its true heritage.

Contents

1 *HISTORY OF THE SIBERIAN HUSKY*

No one knows for certain when people first used dogs to pull sleds. It seems likely that the practice of working dogs in harness originated among the natives of Eurasia. Certainly, Eskimos were using dogs to pull sleds 1,500 years ago but there is evidence that sled dogs date from 4,000 or more years ago. Accompanied by their jackal-type dogs, the people of Central Asia migrated to populate the extremities of Siberia and the Arctic. Their dogs, which were crossbred with the native wolf, developed over time into what became known as the Northern Breeds. From this early group of Northern dogs, the breeds developed their own individual characteristics, which have survived through the ages.

Among these Northern Breeds, the Siberian Husky is probably the best known today.

THE BREED EMERGES

The term husky was originally applied to Eskimos themselves by the Hudson Bay Company's employees. The term

The Siberian Husky is an enigmatic breed that has enchanted people for more than 3,000 years.

husky is a corruption of 'Esky', a slang word for Eskimo.

'Husky' referred to all sled-pulling breeds and implied a dog with a thick coat, a pointed face with prick ears, and a brush tail. When the breed first arrived in North America, in order to differentiate the Northern Siberian dog from the Eskimos' Huskies, they became known as Siberian Huskies and the name has remained with them.

It is thought that the Siberian Husky was originally developed by the Chukchi people of north-eastern Siberia. The Siberian has a long history with this tribe, probably dating back three thousand years or more, and was crucial to their survival and integral to the Chukchi culture. Records are hard to find, since these people did not keep written accounts of their lives, but their lifestyles remained unchanged for decades and centuries at a time, since they did not embrace change readily, and preferred to stick to the established ways.

Their lifestyles were divided into two different types. The inland people kept reindeer, and some of them had village dogs, but these were not the same dogs as those owned by the people living along the Arctic and Pacific coasts in areas which remained unaffected by the Russians until the early 20th century. It was these people who bred the Chukchi sled dogs. The Chukchi were not nomads: they were a village people living in permanent settlements along the Arctic coast. They had been driven there following a series of Russian wars with the Eskimos over control of the Bering Strait. Forced into poorer and poorer hunting grounds, the Chukchi developed a long-distance sled dog breed which needed little food in order to cover huge distances over pack ice to the open sea and the Chukchi hunting grounds and then return to their villages. Thus they developed the breed we know today. They were a fiercely independent people. The Russians had tried to subjugate the Chukchis for centuries – attempting to destroy the race during the mid-1700s. The people survived through their own hardiness and determination and with the help of their dogs, and in 1837 a treaty was signed giving the Chukchi political and cultural independence from Russia.

Their isolation ensured the purity of their dogs and kept their culture unchanged until the middle of the 19th century. It is interesting to note that the small size of the dogs was countered by running large teams; often borrowing dogs from other villagers to make up teams of 16 or 18 dogs when going on a long journey. Many similarities exist between what is known of the Chukchi dogs and our own Siberian Huskies. Their speed, stamina, and ability to cover long distances with minimal energy usage, all reflect today's dogs. Added to this, the males were reserved and dignified, while the bitches were affectionate and intelligent. The dogs often slept in the Chukchi snow houses giving comfort to the children – unlike any of the other Arctic tribes. How many of today's Siberians love to be warm and cosy indoors as well as running and playing out of doors?

Races were not uncommon even at this time and, in 1869, a famous 150-mile challenge between a Russian officer driving a Russian sled dog team and a native Chukchi team was won by a margin of more than an hour by the Chukchi.

SOVIET INTERVENTION

Sadly, the Soviets finally managed to subjugate the Chukchi during the early part of the 20th century by killing the village leaders and breaking down the old tribal systems. Other native people and Russians entered the Chukchi lands bringing with them their own dogs and thus confusing the history of the Siberian Husky. As a result of this it is still maintained in Western literature that the Kolyma region is the source of the Chukchi sled dog. In fact this is extremely unlikely, since the Chukchi people had not bred dogs in this area for centuries.

A further major factor affecting the traceability of the ancestors of the Siberian was a political decision made by the Soviet government. In the 1930s the Soviets, recognising the worth of the sled dog for transport, established a policy which divided all Northern Breeds into four types: sled dogs, game

The Soviets set out to destroy small, native sled dogs.

hunting dogs, reindeer hunting dogs and small game hunting dogs. The Chukchi dog was specifically excluded as being too small for the freighting task which sled dogs were expected to fulfil. In later years, the Soviet government actually banned the breeding of dogs other than those which fell into these categories and claimed that only their draught dogs could lay claim to the title of Siberian Husky.

SAVING THE SIBERIAN HUSKY

The Soviets, during the middle years of the 20th century, systematically destroyed all the small, native sled dog breeds of the various tribes, so it is fortunate that William Goosak and

William Madsen, in the very early years of the century, and, slightly later, Fox Maule Ramsay and Iver Olsen purchased their dogs from the Chukchi people and thus ensured the survival of the breed into the 21st century. The last of the direct imports to the United States were made by Olaf Swenson in 1930. Swenson had an exclusive five-year contract to bring supplies into Siberia and bring furs out and he knew sled dogs well. He recognised the merit of the Chukchi dogs and, when his ship became icebound in October 1929, he travelled 4,500 miles overland to the trans-Siberian railroad, sending his team back to the ship and collecting them the following spring to export to New England. Swenson obtained the best dogs he could. He was aware of the Chukchi culture of caring, harmonious living with their dogs. The Chukchi believed that their dogs guarded the gates to heaven and no one who mistreated a dog would be allowed to enter. So Swenson brought good practice, along with good dogs, to the United States and added greatly to the inheritance of the Siberian Husky that we know today.

THE ALL-ALASKA SWEEPSTAKES

Gold was discovered in Alaska in 1880 and prospectors poured into the area to try to make their fortunes. Few were truly successful but, nonetheless, a hugely increased population needed supplies and transport. The cold weather ensured that areas were cut off from the rest of the world for long periods and the only way in or out was by dog team. These teams were made up from local dogs – local Nordic types – and from large, more southerly dogs with shorter coats and flop ears. Many of these dogs were simply stolen from

Racing sled dogs became popular at the time of the Alaskan Gold Rush.

their owners and taken north. Nome was a town typical of the time, where dogs were essential to the survival of the population, and teams were a source of pride as well as transport. Inevitably, stories grew of the prowess of one team over another and eventually it became obvious that the only way to prove who owned the best team was to race them.

The Nome Kennel Club was founded in 1907 as the organiser and sponsor of the All-Alaska Sweepstakes race. Rules were laid down and a course was chosen. The course ran from Nome to Candle and back – a distance of 408 miles with a wide variety of trail conditions and weather. The race was scheduled for April, so preliminary races were held through the winter to accustom the dogs and drivers to the task ahead.

The first race was held in 1908 and, in the same year William Goosak – a Russian fur-trader – imported a team of small dogs from Siberia. These dogs were so tiny, compared to the customary freighting dogs, that Goosak was laughed at. Driven by a Norwegian named Thurstrup, and against all the odds, the team came in third in the 1909 race – losing out only due to poor tactical decisions on the part of the driver. A young man named Fox Maule Ramsay, a Scottish miner and sportsman, took a liking to the qualities of these relatively small dogs to such an extent that he chartered a schooner and travelled to Siberia the following

summer to purchase some 70 Siberian Huskies, obtained from the small settlement of Markova on the Anadyr River. Ramsay took the dogs back to Nome, along with two native dog handlers. Over a period, interest in the races increased and working harnesses were refined to a lighter racing version, sleds became lighter and the whole enterprise took a more serious turn.

In 1910, Ramsay entered three teams of Siberian Huskies in the race. One, driven by John 'Iron Man' Johnson, won in a record time: 408 miles in 74 hours 14 minutes and 37 seconds, which has never been broken. Ramsay came second. The popularity of the Siberian Husky was set to grow.

THE LEGENDARY SEPPALA
From 1915 to 1917 the All-Alaska Sweepstakes was won by Leonard Seppala with a team of Siberian Huskies. Here was a man who became a legend as the greatest dog-team driver. Seppala, a Norwegian, had gone to Alaska in search of gold at the turn of the century. He became obsessed by sled dog racing following his entry in the 1914 Sweepstakes. He had only taken part following the failure of a trip planned by the explorer Roald Amundsen, leaving Seppala with time, and dogs, on his hands.

The best-known Seppala legend was born in 1925 when he and his team played a critical role in bringing diphtheria serum from Nenana to

Seppala with his team, Ottawa 1931. From right to left: Tserko (left lead); Bonzo (right lead); Kreevanka (left point); Bijou; followed by Smokey, Matte and Kingeak. Courtesy: Dale and Nancy Wolfe, Ohio.

Nome. An outbreak of diphtheria in Nome early in the year led to a shortage of antitoxin, with the nearest supply in Anchorage. This could be transported by train as far as Nenana but it was impossible to take it further other than by sled dog team. It was agreed to use relays of teams to speed the transport outwards from Nenana while Seppala drove towards the arriving team. On meeting the team coming out with the serum, Seppala turned and raced back to Nome – a risky and difficult journey fraught with danger. His and his fellow driver's bravery, and the speed and stamina of the dogs, averted a diphtheria epidemic and they were hailed as heroes. Seppala's most famous lead dog was Togo, his race leader for many years and leader during what became known as the serum run.

After the serum run, Seppala toured the east coast of the United States with his Siberian teams, winning as they had in Alaska. Seppala's achievements were instrumental in promoting the Siberian Husky as a breed across America.

The Siberian Husky was officially recognised by the American Kennel Club in 1930, with the first Breed Standard being published in 1932. The Siberian Husky Club of America was founded in 1938.

THE SIBERIAN IN THE UK
Although the recent development of the Siberian in the UK stems largely from the early 1970s, Huskies are recorded as being kept in this country over a century before. It is not certain whether these were Siberians, or other types of Husky, but they are certainly very similar in appearance to the modern-day Siberian Husky. These dogs spent the majority of their lives in zoos, rarely being seen at shows. Exceptions to this were Huskies owned by two collectors of foreign breeds, Mr W.K. Taunton and Mr H.C. Brook, who imported a few towards the end of the 19th century.

Taunton's best dog was named Sir John Franklin and he won many awards during 1879-81. He sired several litters out of Zoe, a bitch bred from Huskies owned by the London Zoological Society. Mr Brooke's dogs included Arctic King, who is said to have been typical but on the small side at 22 inches, and Farthest North, a larger dog at 25-26 inches, and well marked. Huskies failed to gain popularity, possibly due to stories of their alleged ferocity – a reputation which is still mentioned on occasion by those who have yet to be beguiled by the sweet nature of the Siberian! In slightly more recent years, a Husky named Angugssuak, also owned by the London Zoological Society, was exhibited fairly regularly and appeared at Crufts in both 1938 and 1939.

The Siberian Husky has continued to grow in popularity and has spread throughout the world. The history of the breed in different countries is covered further in later chapters.

The Siberian's worldwide popularity has gone from strength to strength.

2 *CHOOSING YOUR SIBERIAN HUSKY*

T he Siberian Husky is a victim of its own good looks. Most people are attracted by their stunning appearance and happy disposition but, essentially, Siberian Huskies do not make good pets for everyone. The hunting instinct in the Siberian is still strong – just one look is enough to see how closely they resemble their wolf ancestors – and the instinct to hunt, while important to many breeds, is in the forefront of the minds of most Siberians. Of course there are exceptions, the dogs who would never dream of leaving their owner's side, let alone chasing the neighbour's rabbit or cat but, for the majority, it is essential that they are kept on the lead or safely contained at all times.

Siberians can be obedience-trained but they just are not the first choice for someone who wants to take the sport seriously. They have other thoughts on their minds and anyone with a cat, or any other small pet, would be strongly

Siberian Husky pups are irresistible – but think long and hard before taking one on as a companion.

advised to look elsewhere. Siberians love people and get on well with other dogs but they like each other's company best. That is what makes them such a delight to keep as a group.

Kept as single pets, they need plenty of human attention and would prefer not to be left alone all day waiting for their owner to get back from work. Unfortunately, they may tend to 'ask questions later' when it comes to small dogs. To the Siberian, at a glance, a small dog or puppy can be just like a cat or a rabbit, so it is advisable to make introductions over a period and not to leave a Siberian alone with a vulnerable smaller pet.

Add to all this the fact that the Siberian Husky is an excellent digger, and you will see why they do not make the ideal pet for everyone. If you like your garden, you will have to get used to the idea of keeping your Husky out of it and safely secured in his own area. To do this, you need a concrete run with high, welded, mesh fencing: hedges, wooden fences and chain link are all just too easy to get through, under or over.

THE RIGHT PRIORITIES

The Siberian Husky comes in a variety of 'types'. Which one you choose may well be dictated by what you have in mind for your dog and where you live. Do you want to show your dog? Do you want to run him in harness? Do you want to compete in races or just run your dog for exercise? Do you want your dog purely as a pet? Or do you want to do everything?

Before all other considerations, you must want your dog as a pet. Whether you work or show your Siberian, there may come a time when either you or the dog loses interest in the hobby side of things either due to age, waning interest or lack of time.

Whatever the situation, your dog will still need a loving home, food and exercise, so never take on a dog simply because you want to take part in a sport: if you want the dog for himself, everything else is a bonus. Equally, steer well clear of any breeder who advertises 'work/show homes only'. Breeders, too, should place more importance on the long-term stability of the pup's future home, so go for the breeder who is more interested in you rather than whether you want to compete.

So, to return to 'type'. In some countries, it is possible to buy a dog which will be able to perform on the trail and in the show ring with equal success. In other countries, the breed has been split into 'show' and 'work' types and you will have to choose accordingly. If you are not interested in either, then you have the freedom to choose but, remember, the Siberian Husky Standard does not call for a particular coat or eye colour and some breeders do not like puppy buyers to request a particular coat pattern or eye colour. Siberians are not 'born to order'. They come as they are and, in any case, their coat colour and pattern changes over time and, if you look back at photos of your puppy in years to come, you will see a very different-looking dog.

DOG OR BITCH?

So do you want a male or a female? This is very much personal preference and people often choose on the basis of the dogs they lived with as a child. Any discussion on the relative merits of one sex over the other is bound to be full of generalisations, so bear this in mind.

Males are bigger and stronger and so may be more difficult to control on the lead. Females can be more 'sparky' with their fellow Siberians and may be rather more 'hunt oriented'. Both sexes, while allowing for individual variation, are affectionate and enjoy attention but will usually wait for you to come to them rather than seeking you out.

Females come into season, while males have an annoying tendency to lift their legs on other people's cars – not popular if you live in a built-up neighbourhood.

Neutering tends to ruin coats so do not believe people who say you can choose either sex and then just have them neutered. Consider putting your female 'on the pill' if seasons are really a nuisance.

PUPPY OR ADULT?

Most people think in terms of buying a puppy when they consider getting a dog but, while there are advantages to this, there are also advantages to getting an adult. Siberians come up for rehoming on a regular basis – mostly because people have not thought carefully enough about the commitment they are making and the specific needs of the Siberian Husky. Other reasons for rehoming are common to other breeds – marriage breakdown, the arrival of a new baby, moving to unsuitable accommodation etc. None of these reasons are the fault of the dog; in fact, it is rare that Siberians are put up for rehoming as a result of

Choosing a dog or a bitch is a matter of personal preference.

poor temperament – they just behave like Siberians, not Labradors. So taking on an adult is not as 'risky' as it might be with another breed.

The advantage of taking on a puppy is that you can mould him to your way of life right from the start. Set against that is the fact that puppies need training which takes time, and they generally need more attention – requiring more frequent feeding and lots of play, and of course they need to be house-trained.

The rescued adult will generally already be house-trained (and even ex-kennel dogs learn their house-training extremely quickly) and will usually be more affectionate than the average adult, since he has now found himself in an attentive home. If you know the dog's history, you will also know whether or not he is accustomed to children and to other pets, which can be an advantage. You also need to know if there are any other 'problem' areas with the dog – this would be unusual for Siberians, but well worth knowing about beforehand.

PREPARING FOR YOUR DOG

A new puppy or adult will need a bed. A hard plastic one with a nylon fur liner is best, as it is more difficult to chew. Old-fashioned baskets and modern beanbags are easily destroyed and may cause harm if the pieces are swallowed. Two pieces of nylon fur will give you the opportunity to have one in the wash at all times!

Water and food bowls – metal ones are safest for the same reason as the bed – a

collar and lead (which will need to be replaced as the puppy grows), plus an extending lead, and a brush and comb, are the basics. 'Slicker' brushes are very effective on Siberian coats but you should choose the soft version, the tips of which are rounded and much more gentle on the skin. You should run any grooming equipment over the back of your hand before using it on your dog – if it hurts you, then do not use it. A fairly wide-toothed metal comb is also effective, mostly for cleaning out the brush while you are grooming, but it can also be used on the longer fur around the trousers and on the tail. Remember, though, that most dogs hate their tails being groomed. The tail is the extension of the dog's spine, so you must handle it with care.

In addition, a crate or cage is very useful, particularly for house-training your puppy or for introducing the new

Make sure fences and gates are secure before bringing your pup home.

addition to dogs already in the household. The value of a crate for keeping a dog safe while you are busy concentrating on other things cannot be overemphasised. Obviously, no dog should be made to sit in a crate for hours on end but, if you train your puppy to be used to a crate, you will reap the rewards for many years to come. Crate-training is discussed elsewhere in this book.

Before you bring your Siberian home, you must ensure that you have either a purpose-built run ready or that your garden is securely fenced. Again, this is discussed elsewhere in this book but do not leave this until after the puppy arrives – puppies can wriggle out through the smallest of holes and an adult Siberian will scale a five-foot fence, or dig under one, with ease.

CHOOSING A PUPPY

Try to visit the litter of puppies when they are a few weeks old – breeders vary in how soon they like visitors, since they may disturb the bitch. In any case, puppies are not particularly interesting until they reach at least three weeks, since they are fairly static and have not yet started to play much. Four to six weeks is best, at which time you can discuss with the breeder what will suit your household. We have already covered the subject of male or female and of colouring, but temperament is extremely important and it can be possible to tell how lively or 'sparky' a puppy will be as he grows up from his behaviour towards

A litter is usually visited for the first time between three to six weeks. This pup is three weeks old.

his siblings.

The breeder will be able to judge which puppy will suit you best or may give you the choice from a couple of puppies. At least one puppy should be staying with the breeder and others may already be booked, so do not feel disappointed if you are not offered a choice from the whole litter.

In Siberians, it is not easy to choose which puppy may be 'pick of the litter'. This term is used mostly in show circles for the puppy which looks most likely to do well in the show ring. Siberians change so much as they grow and, indeed, they do not mature fully until three years of age. The outstanding puppy can, therefore, be very difficult to spot and, unlike other breeds, because there is so much variation in 'type', there may be more than one 'pick' in the litter.

Puppies change so much as they develop that it is difficult to spot one with show or working potential.

An experienced breeder can usually pick out the most likely puppies for the show ring but, for a good working dog, attitude for running is inherited, so the litter should be very similar, providing they are properly trained.

REGISTRATIONS
When you collect your puppy, the breeder will give you a copy of the pedigree and should also give you a signed document to transfer the puppy from the breeder's name to your own. Once you have completed this transfer document, it should be sent to the issuing authority such as The Kennel Club in the UK or the American Kennel Club etc. A new document will be issued to you, showing that the puppy is now recorded as being owned by you.

Depending on the country, this document may also include particular

stipulations or 'endorsements' relating to what you may do with the puppy. For instance, in the UK, a breeder may endorse the registration so that an Export Pedigree cannot be issued without the breeder's consent. In this way, the breeder can keep track of the dog and know if you plan to take him or her abroad. Any such endorsements must be fully explained to the puppy buyer at the time of sale and, under normal circumstances, they will be lifted by the breeder at the owner's request.

PEDIGREES
Pedigrees usually show either three generations of the puppy's ancestors or five generations. It will depend on how interested you are in the subject as to whether you specifically request a longer pedigree. They take a long time to compile but, in some countries, it is possible to ask the registering body to reproduce pedigrees from the records that are kept on all registered dogs.

It is advisable to study some pedigrees, or to ask those already in the breed for information on dogs and whether they have been worked or what they have achieved either on the trail or in the ring. Using a successful working Siberian at stud does not guarantee good working pups but it does increase the likelihood. Whether or not you plan to compete with your Siberian, you will still find it interesting to look into your puppy's ancestry. Siberian Huskies, in common with all breeds, suffer from inherited conditions and it is wise to consider these and discover everything you can before committing yourself to a companion who will be around, hopefully, for the next fifteen or more years. See the chapter on Health for more information on hereditary breed conditions but, here again, it is advisable to study pedigrees and ask for advice before 'diving in'.

In many pedigrees you will see evidence of line breeding, which is the mating of related dogs within a line or family to a common ancestor: in other words, the same dogs appear a number of times within a pedigree. Less commonly you will see inbreeding, which is the mating of close relatives, for instance, father to daughter. Both these techniques are used by breeders to 'fix' desirable traits (such as a good running attitude, or good conformation) in the offspring. However, inbreeding in particular may also bring to the surface undesirable traits. This practice therefore should only be carried out by knowledgeable breeders and should only be used where lines are known to be clear of hereditary defects. Out-crossing to unrelated lines is advisable if the hereditary position is not known or is unclear.

COLOUR AND COAT

It is common to see Siberians with two differently-coloured eyes, or even eyes of split colour, part blue and part brown. This variation is part of the Siberian's charm. In many breeds, the need to conform to a particular coat colour, shading or pattern of markings, and to maintain a particular depth of eye colour, means that these characteristics are often placed ahead of conformation and movement. Clearly, in a breed of this type, this would not be in the best interests of the dog's working ability, so colour and pattern have never been given any importance in the Siberian ideal.

The same cannot be said of coat and coat quality. While this is not given undue importance in the Breed Standard, it is nevertheless true that a Siberian with an over-long or 'woolly' coat is at a disadvantage for working, since overheating is common when pulling at speed or for a long distance.

This is not a problem for the 'pet' home or for anyone interested in competing in obedience, but it would not be advisable for those wishing to work or show their Siberian. That said, it is one of the most attractive coats and those who own them hold 'woollies' in great affection. Bear in mind, though, that they take more grooming and need greater care to maintain – it is unwise to neuter these dogs or the coat will become truly impossible.

The most usual colours are grey and white, black and white and, less common, red and white. Piebalds and solid colours do occur but, apart from solid white, these usually have white markings on the face. The 'dirty face' is coloured and has little white – the most wolf-like patterning in the Siberian. Blue and brown are the most common eye colours but these vary greatly in shade from ice white to deep blue and from tan to dark brown.

If you have an ideal colour and pattern of markings in mind, set it aside when you go to see the litter from which you hope to have a puppy. Bear in mind that the Siberian's markings will change over time: black markings around the eyes, on a white face, will fade by the time the puppy is a year or two old and photos of the same dog taken just a year or so apart show some amazing changes.

Siberian puppies come in a wide variety of colours and markings.

TAKING YOUR PUPPY HOME

So you have chosen your puppy and it is time to collect him and take him home. The breeder will have let you know how old the puppy will be when you collect him. Opinions differ; some believe that puppies should go as early as possible, even at six weeks, suggesting that this gives more opportunity for early socialising and getting to know the new environment. Many believe that this is too young, particularly for a pack animal which learns so much about good behaviour from his mother. For this reason, we prefer to keep puppies until 10 weeks.

Travelling home can be stressful for the puppy, but most Siberians take to car travel well. The breeder may have taken the pups out once or twice in a vehicle, either for vaccinations or just to accustom them to the car, in which case the pup will be less concerned. If you are travelling alone, you will need to take a crate to put the puppy in safely for the return journey. This is advisable even if you have other people in the car with you, since the puppy will need to sleep on a longer journey or to be contained when you get out of the car for any reason. Taking a piece of bedding along for the puppies to play with together before you travel home is a good idea, since this will give your puppy something to cuddle up to which smells familiar.

If you have a long journey home you will need to make 'comfort' stops. Make sure you are well away from the road and that the puppy's collar is secure. A small harness is even better under these circumstances since harnesses are much more difficult to slip out of.

3 OWNING A SIBERIAN HUSKY

Before the arrival of a new puppy, you should reflect on the young animal you are taking on. You will direct his entire life from puppyhood, through puberty, adolescence, adulthood and into old age. This is a sobering thought and should remind you that you are taking on a serious responsibility for another life.

Ask yourself what you want from this puppy. Is he going to grow into a family pet, an individual companion, a show dog, a racing dog or all of these?

In most cases your puppy was chosen because he was the most beautiful and sweet-natured puppy in the world, so surely he deserves the best.

CARING FOR YOUR PUPPY
From the moment you bring your puppy home, make him welcome and introduce him to his new world. He will need a bed, toys, a bowl of water and an area safe from dangers, where he can

From the moment your puppy arrives home, you are responsible for all his needs.

play and investigate at will. Initially it will all be strange to him, particularly as he will have just left his mother and his brothers and sisters. His whole life is upset, so he needs reassurance that his surroundings are safe. It will be best for him if the first 24 hours are kept as calm as possible to let him get used to his new home. Save the excitement of new introductions for a day or so. Puppies are very resilient and are changing constantly so, within a few days, your Siberian puppy will be feeling happy and well adjusted to his new environment. Then will be the time to expand his world.

Regular trips out to the garden will make house-training quick and simple.

HOUSE-TRAINING

Old-fashioned methods of house-training are just that – old-fashioned. House-training is relatively easy to achieve without any newspaper, nose-rubbing or telling off. Just work with the puppy and be ahead of the game rather than trying to correct his actions.

As soon as the puppy has settled into his new home, begin a policy of showing him where he is to relieve himself. If he is to go in the garden, then carry him outside as soon as he wakes up. Supervise and praise him as soon as he performs. It is important not to simply put the puppy outside and leave him to it – he will probably sit on the back doorstep and wait for you to let him back in, then go on the carpet. So stay with him until he has been, then bring him back indoors and repeat the process every hour, after every meal and every time he wakes up.

You will gradually be able to lengthen the time between visits outside as his bladder develops and he gains more control. It can take anything between six months and a year to get a puppy fully house-trained, so do not expect miracles and do not tell him off if you forget to put him outside. Males tend to house-train more quickly than females but there are always exceptions.

It will not take long for you to recognise when he is likely to need to go out, and he will quickly learn to ask you to let him out by glancing at the back door, so watch for the signs.

Dogs prefer to relieve themselves in specific areas and will choose their own spot if left without guidance. The problem comes when this does not tie in with your plans, particularly if the puppy has taught himself to go somewhere in the house. It can then be very hard to change this behaviour.

Dogs that live in kennels or, as many Siberians do, in large packs in a compound, will learn to use one area and thus limit the space which is accessible for them to lie in or play in.

SOCIALISATION

It is important to socialise your puppy as early and as often as possible. Supervise all introductions. Let him meet family members, friends and anyone who comes to the house. "Would you like to see the new puppy?" is an invitation which is almost universally accepted and provides yet another opportunity for your puppy to expand his knowledge of the world and to meet new and varied people.

Try to introduce your puppy at an early age to all the sounds you can. A dog that is frightened of the noise from a vacuum cleaner, a loud thunderclap or a lawn mower, will prove difficult to live with in later life. Try to understand your puppy's needs. He is led by his instincts and has inherited a desire to investigate and to learn about the world. His nose and his mouth are his main learning tools: allow him to bite and chew toys. Be patient if items you had not wished to be used in that way also become 'toys' – he cannot know the difference, so keep precious items out of reach.

THE SLEEPING AREA

Providing your puppy with his own sleeping place is also important. Siberian Huskies are generally extremely friendly, but even though they will greet humans with glee and happily accept affection, they are fundamentally a reserved breed. Siberians need an area to retreat to – a corner, a high ledge or platform in the garden will suit many dogs. He may well appreciate a hiding place – his den – to retire to.

If you keep just one or two Siberians, they will probably spend most of their time indoors. Providing they are well exercised, Siberians are very calm in the house, usually retiring for a nap until something interesting happens. The only drawback to having them indoors is the amount of moulting that many of them do. Regular grooming and use of the vacuum cleaner easily controls this problem. The Husky's coat does not smell, particularly if he is bathed two or three times a year, and the dog's calm nature and lack of panting or fretting in the house, make him a good house pet, with very little in the way of clumsy damage or slobbery stains.

LEAD-TRAINING

Choose a small, buckle-type collar that fits not too tightly but not so loosely that the puppy can chew it or get his teeth into the loop in a way that could trap his mouth. This collar should be worn in the house by the puppy for a short time and then removed. This

Lead-training is essential for the Siberian puppy.

process can be repeated at intervals until the puppy is accustomed to wearing it and to having it put on and taken off. If you play with him as soon as you have put the collar on, he will associate the collar with having a good time. Try to ensure that he either sits or stands still while the collar is put on – the excitement should come afterwards.

It is equally important to ensure that your puppy enjoys the experience when he is first introduced to a lead. He should be allowed to play while wearing his collar and then encouraged to walk towards you while you hold the lead loosely. Let the puppy lead you around to start with, so that he does not feel restricted. Gradually, he will come to accept the collar and lead as your means of letting him know where he is to go and, as he will mostly want to be with you, it will also give him the confidence of being able to stay close to you.

Remember that the lead is more than just a means of restricting and directing. It is also a means of communication, through which the puppy receives information about your moods.

TYPES OF COLLARS

As the puppy gets older, you will need to increase the size of the collar and also choose one that is suitable for his strength. Siberians, even when they have been taught to walk properly at heel, still have enormous, and unexpected, strength if they suddenly see something which they want to get hold of quickly – a cat or rabbit, for example. It is no good discovering at that particular moment that your dog's collar cannot withstand a sudden jerk!

Choose a fairly wide (3/4 inch) nylon buckle collar. The collar buckle and lead snap should be solid brass as this is strong and will not freeze in the winter when you are trying to undo it on a frozen morning. Check chains are definitely 'out' for the Siberian (except in experienced hands in the show ring)

Tracking harnesses are useful when teaching your pup to walk on the lead.

Chewing relieves boredom and helps with a puppy's teething.

and even half-checks are inadvisable. In some countries, any tightening movement in the collar is against the rules of competition for dogs in race teams and, in most circumstances, the fixed buckle collar is the most suitable for Siberians. The collar should be fitted so that you can get at least two fingers between it and the dog's neck, but remember that Siberians are very good at wriggling backwards out of a collar, so do not have it too loose either.

Tracking harnesses, again made from fairly wide nylon webbing, are a useful alternative to collars if you walk your Husky in a built-up area, since you can have confidence that he cannot slip out of it if startled by traffic, for instance. Once again, fit is important and you should choose a harness which is adjustable and fits snugly without rubbing.

CHEWING

The natural instinct for a dog to chew is strongest during puppyhood. Chewing aids the development of both teeth and jaws, and relieves gums irritated by teething. Occasionally, milk teeth may not fall out even once the adult teeth

have grown through – seek advice from your vet if this occurs.

For puppies, chewing is both a game and a way to discover the world. You should ensure that the puppy has plenty of suitable toys for chewing and play. Strong rubber toys are excellent, but anything that can be swallowed, such as soft 'squeaky' toys, should not be given to either adults or puppies. Tennis balls are not suitable since they can be broken up and swallowed, but large chunks of firewood provide endless amusement and make good toys.

It is equally important to provide toys for adults since these relieve boredom and avoid the alternative, which is that your dog will find his own, less suitable, items – such as the furniture – to chew. Chewing by adults is normal and healthy, although the level of chewing will vary greatly from dog to dog.

Chewing can remove tartar from teeth and it prevents the accumulation of tartar if the dog has constant access to suitable material to chew.

SAFETY PRECAUTIONS

Modern homes generally have an

abundance of electric power cables which are potentially lethal if they are left plugged in with an unsupervised puppy playing nearby. Stones and pebbles are equally dangerous since they can become lodged in the gut and cause untold damage if swallowed. Always be aware of what your puppy may be able to get hold of and thus avoid problems. Equally, it is well worthwhile keeping a watchful eye on your puppy's faeces (or lack of them), as this will provide a useful indicator to general health and what non-food items may have been eaten.

Dogs that are bored or simply 'passing the time' will chew most things. Many plastic or metal items can be dangerous if swallowed and toxic items abound in our modern world. An uncontrolled dog can be injured investigating your interesting home, so provide mental and physical exercise: suitable chew toys, walks, trips in the car and visits to friends are all good ways to keep your dog happy.

PUPPIES WITH ADULT DOGS
If your puppy is to become part of a household that already has a number of dogs, then gradual introduction to the pack is important. Siberian puppies have a natural, and seemingly urgent, need to relate both physically and mentally to adult dogs. They will seek them out and then be immediately submissive.

The response of the adult Siberian will vary from dog to dog, but will generally be wary and 'standoffish'. An adult female will probably be aware that 'Mum' may be nearby and may be protective of her youngsters. Most adult females will be vocal, warning the puppy to stay away and, for the most part, will try to distance themselves from the newcomer. The adult male Siberian will either be totally disinterested or will try to dominate the puppy, all according to the dog's own position in the pack. 'Putting the pup in its place' is a potentially dangerous situation for both the puppy and the pack, since a yell of pain or fear from the puppy can result in a mass attack from the adults. For this reason it is *essential* never to leave young puppies

Siberian pups like to spend time with adult dogs.

After calm, careful introductions, a pup and an adult Siberian can enjoy a fun relationship together.

unsupervised with adult pack members, even for a few minutes.

Some adults, often the older ones, will enjoy playing with the puppy and, as this relationship develops, a more relaxed atmosphere will be created during these introductory periods. The most important aspect of this time is supervision but do not interfere unless the puppy is in danger. The puppy will learn more by being allowed to play and become accustomed to the adults if he does so without too much 'help' from you. Gradually, all the adults will come to accept the puppy and will establish a routine of play and rest to allow them to live happily together.

OTHER NON-CANINE PETS

Generally, Siberians are not the best breed to keep with other, non-canine, pets, although a single dog can learn to live with a cat or other pet, providing that they are introduced while the

Siberian is young and that the cats do not run from the Siberian once he is an adult. The instinct to chase and kill is very strong in most Siberians and they are not aware that they are chasing a 'friend' if the cat races down the garden. There are exceptions but they are few and far between.

If your Siberian is an only dog, or living with perhaps just one other, ensure that the puppy meets as many other dogs as possible in order that he becomes well socialised. Supervise these meetings to ensure the puppy's safety and observe his reactions to others, which will give you a good indication of your puppy's future character. Problems relating to aggression, dominance etc. can be acted upon, and training undertaken to correct possible future difficulties. In the single-dog household this is an important consideration, as it is the pack situation which tends to correct problems through its hierarchical nature.

BASIC TRAINING

During the early part of your Siberian Husky's life, patterns of behaviour will become established and it is important that you recognise what you will find acceptable once he is an adult. A little puppy jumping at your face to lick you seems very endearing but it will not be so welcome when, as an adult, the dog knocks your glasses off or scratches your face in his excitement to greet you. Curbing potentially annoying and unsociable habits while the dog is young is important because the adult will not understand why behaviour which you found acceptable one day is suddenly frowned upon the next.

Training clubs can give you invaluable help and guidance, but the basic training that your dog requires for a well-adjusted life depends on your constant efforts to implement what you have both learned. Consistency is all-important. Be careful not to confuse him by allowing him to do at home something that is unacceptable at the training club. Anything you expect of him during training should be expected of him at all other times, whether that is not jumping up, or sitting before you cross the road. Your consistency and patience will be rewarded.

The training club also offers the opportunity for a trip out. Your dog should learn that, every time you take him out on his collar and lead, good things happen and, indeed, the trip in the car to the training club is an adventure in itself. Your dog will travel more happily if he has his own secure area, with a sound surface that stops him sliding about with the car's movement. Travelling to the training club safely, and having a good time at the end of a short journey, will help him to accept longer journeys with ease.

Many owners show and race their dogs successfully. The training involved for these occupations is different, and may even be contradictory, but Siberians can differentiate according to circumstance. The dog that pulls hard and constantly in harness is the same dog that walks by your side on a loose lead, or displays his beautiful outline to the judge by standing still and proudly. The results of training are what you see in the dogs around you – both good and bad.

"SIT" AND "STAY"

Even if you have no intention of showing or doing formal Obedience work with your dog, it is good to teach the basics of "Sit" and "Stay". These can prove invaluable and Siberians are quick, if somewhat stubborn, learners. It is true that when you call most Siberians, they are quite likely to jump about playfully, run in the opposite direction or lie down rather than come to you, but they do know what you mean! Teaching Siberians is a simple matter of repetition and reward. Use the same commands at all times and always reward desired behaviour, even if it is just with a pat and a "Good dog". Offering a small treat works even better! As with training 'turn' commands on the trail, it can be as simple as waiting for the puppy to sit, saying "Sit" immediately and then rewarding the puppy for doing what you have apparently just told him to do! He will soon learn that doing as he is told is worthwhile. Gradually, you can reduce the number of occasions when you give a treat until you are simply rewarding with praise. Do not bore your puppy by doing too much training at once – it is better to work on the basis of little and often.

THE HUNTING INSTINCT

No amount of training will alter the fact that your Siberian has a deep-rooted

The Siberian is a natural hunter.

hunting instinct. He may be lying quietly, or playing, and then will suddenly leap up to catch and kill a prey. It is perhaps this sharply-focused hunting instinct that makes the Siberian such a successful sled dog, where the hunting instinct is harnessed to pull.

Your pet Siberian will be no different to any team dog when it comes to the neighbour's cat, a small dog, or a rabbit, and this can lead to, at best, an awkward situation and, at worst, an incident which may be distressing for you and a danger to your dog – particularly as in many countries the law now states that an out-of-control dog may be destroyed. Keeping control of your dog in the modern social environment is essential for good human relationships, and for your dog's health and wellbeing.

THE MULTIFUNCTIONAL HUSKY

Working and showing Siberians are covered in depth elsewhere in this book, but this breed is truly multifunctional and generally enjoys whatever entertainment you like to dream up!

While Siberians may not be the first choice for the serious Obedience competitor, they are nonetheless quick to learn and extremely agile. If they put their mind to it, they can be very good at both Obedience and Agility but they need patience. The Siberian's natural exuberance surfaces at the most awkward of moments and will result in the dog racing joyfully round the ring and loving the resulting laughter! There

The Siberian may not be the first choice as an Obedience dog, but he is a fast learner who enjoys training.

are many training clubs which you can join to see how you get on.

Puppy socialising classes are excellent for introducing puppies to the world and these are generally held by training classes or at veterinary surgeries. At the same time you can teach your puppy the basics of "Sit", "Down" and "Stay" as early as possible. Most Obedience classes will not accept puppies before the age of six months, so you can get some early training in at home.

Agility usually follows on from Obedience training but, again, you will need a local class unless you have your own equipment at home. In any case, this activity is best learned under experienced handlers.

Siberians have been trained to a high standard in both these disciplines

so, even if you are unable to work your dog in harness and do not fancy the show ring, you can still compete with your dog and enjoy yourselves together.

GENERAL HEALTH

Vaccination and worming, flea control, and food quality are dealt with in other chapters, but, as a dog owner, you have to consider other aspects of your dog's welfare.

Set yourself a time for a regular, routine 'check over' for your dog. Look at his ears: are they clean inside, do they show signs of wax build-up or is he scratching them a lot? Are his eyes clear, with no discharge and no staining on the fur below his eyes? Are his teeth in good condition? Check for tartar build-up at the base of a tooth or any sign of cracked or damaged teeth. Is he walking soundly and with his normal gait? Even a slight limp may indicate a sore pad, or a thorn or grass seed stuck in his foot, or a damaged muscle in his leg or shoulder. Run your hands over his body. Feel the shape beneath his coat: is he fat underneath that coat or is his weight below normal? You should be able to feel his ribs clearly and he should be lean but not thin. You may find a tick or a 'hot spot' of wet eczema that you had not noticed before.

Keep an eye on his stools because these can tell you a lot about his general state of health. Loose motions are not uncommon in Siberians and can be a result of overfeeding. If your dog is

Your Siberian should be checked over regularly to keep him in tip-top condition.

underweight, build him up gradually through a few small meals rather than one large one. The Siberian Husky is a lighter-built dog than its appearance suggests. Food intake is therefore lower than some people would expect, particularly if the dog is fed on a dry complete diet. Siberians can be very diet-sensitive and a sudden change in either type or quantity of food can have a significant effect. Checking your dog's body 'cover' and stool quality will guide you to the correct amount of food for him.

While on the subject of stools, eating faeces is common among dogs of all ages – particularly puppies. Many dogs grow out of the habit but it is a significant factor in continuing the worm cycle, so be diligent in clearing up after your dog quickly.

PUPPY FOOD
For your puppy, choose a Puppy or Junior food with a medium bite size that requires him to chew his food and not to bolt it down. Once he reaches nine months or so, change to an adult food, preferably a top-of-the-range diet for active dogs – particularly if you intend to run your dog in harness. Make any change gradually over a few days to avoid upsets. You should continue feeding puppy quantities until your pup is a year old and only then switch to using the adult feeding guide.

Dogs thrive on routine, and treats should be just that – a treat and not part of the main diet. If you follow this course, you can use treats to help with training. Perhaps a small biscuit at night before you turn out the light will help your puppy to accept this part of his routine. A small treat for coming when called is also a good idea, particularly for Siberians who can be exceptionally stubborn on this point!

Siberians need routine, particularly when it comes to feeding.

THE ADULT APPETITE

Exercise level, temperature and age all play a part in deciding how much food your dog will eat. Siberians are not naturally big eaters, and the times when they refuse food, particularly with males, should not be a cause for alarm. A single dog will not eat as enthusiastically as one in a pack, since the element of competition is absent. Providing your dog is healthy and cheerful, any lack of appetite will usually only last for a day or two. Occasionally, particularly within packs, it can indicate a 'bug'. Recovery from this type of thing is usually quite rapid but if you are worried, seek veterinary advice.

Males will also lose their desire to eat if a bitch comes into season nearby. This, again, is quite normal and may continue for some time. Other behavioural changes in this situation may include aggression towards other males, tension and stress in the pack together with the most heart-rending of howls (especially in the quiet of the night). This is all designed to try your patience but, as the dogs are simply responding instinctively, it is unfair to treat them other than with understanding.

THE BALANCED DIET

The diet you feed will depend on a number of different factors including age, activity and health. For the majority, feeding a good-quality complete dry food offers both

Siberians can lose their appetites in warm weather.

convenience and confidence that you are feeding a nutritionally complete and balanced diet suited to your dog's needs. There are fewer than half a dozen truly top-quality feeds on the market, so you need to look beyond the advertiser's claims to find the best.

Other types of food available include canned, semi-moist and fresh and frozen foods. Fresh and frozen meats need to be mixed with biscuit, and vitamins must be added to make up a complete diet, so they have obvious drawbacks although dogs love them! Canned and semi-moist foods may be complete or may need additions. Check the packaging as to whether the food is 'complete' or 'complementary'. Complementary foods require the addition of other ingredients in order to make up a balanced diet. The disadvantage to these foods is the quantity required to feed, since a high proportion of the food is moisture. With a dry food the dog gets his water intake from the water bowl, although many people like to add water at the time of feeding. Once again, dogs love canned foods and many people choose to add a little to a complete dry food – not actually necessary but it makes the owner feel that they are giving their dog a tastier meal!

If you choose to use dry foods, bear in mind that there are two different types: extruded (pellet/nugget style) and flake (muesli style). Top-quality foods of either type are suitable but you should avoid the cheaper flake foods. The digestive system of the dog is unable to digest raw starch and these foods contain it in abundance, hence the undigested flakes and cereals that appear on the lawn! You have to feed more in order to make up for the indigestibility of the food, so they are simply a false economy and not the best thing for your dog. Siberians tend to have quite sensitive digestive systems and good-quality extruded foods, preferably wheat gluten-free, seem to suit best, causing far less upset and leading to happier, healthier dogs.

Foods have become more and more sophisticated over recent years and you will find diets directed at different life stages and mouth sizes along with foods for highly active dogs and for fatties.

FOOD QUANTITY

The question of feeding quantity is simply addressed and you should sort this out for yourself rather than relying on the manufacturer's recommendations, since these are a guide not a fixed quantity. Base your initial quantity on the guide given on the packaging. You can then alter the amount fed over time, as you see how your puppy develops. Your dog should be lean and well muscled without being thin, at all times, so, if he starts to become either underweight or overweight, you should adjust the feeding quantity accordingly. Do not make large changes in quantity, do it gradually, as a sudden large increase will almost always result in diarrhoea.

You can judge your dog's weight and condition by running your hands over his backbone and ribs to check that they are

Sometimes your Siberian may choose his own diet – blackberries are a favourite snack.

33

well covered but with no sign of fat. You should be able to feel the bones clearly but without 'dipping' between the ribs. Have in your mind the image of a human athlete – you will never see a successful human runner whose ribs do not show. However, making the judgement between lean and thin is important, as no dog should be emaciated but neither should he be overweight. Dogs are much happier if they are able to run around and remain fit rather than being overfed simply because the owner could not resist the wonderful show of begging which dogs are so good at! You have a responsibility to keep your dog fit and healthy and you should treat it as one of the most important aspects of looking after your dog.

Treats can make up part of your dog's diet but make sure that any treats you give are kept to a minimum and do not get out of hand. Giving treats can be very

An adult Siberian will enjoy two meals a day.

helpful for training, particularly for puppies, but you should adjust the amount you feed if necessary.

Feeding puppies is covered in the chapter on breeding but, as a general rule, you should give four meals a day up to twelve weeks old, three meals up to six months and two meals a day thereafter. Feeding twice a day for all dogs is better for them, if less convenient for you, since it means they have a smaller amount of food to digest at one time. Eating all our daily food requirements in one meal would leave us feeling overfull at the time and hungry later on in the day, and the same applies to your dog.

FOOD BOWLS
Food bowls vary from plastic, to china, to metal and stoneware. Bear in mind that a puppy will delight in playing with his bowl so you are better off choosing something unbreakable. Plastic can be chewed, so most Siberian owners use metal bowls. These get battered around over the years but do stand the tests of time and teeth!

THE SIBERIAN'S COAT
Your Siberian Husky comes well equipped for most extremes of weather. His dense double coat is the ultimate protection against icy-cold winds and drifting snow. This same coat offers a remarkable barrier to water and it is not uncommon to see Siberians lying out in the rain seemingly unaware of the weather. A quick shake, and a few

minutes later the coat is dry and has returned to normal. Rain hardly penetrates the dense coat so the skin remains dry. A quick towel-down will have him back indoors, without ruining your furniture, in minutes.

The only exception to this is in puppies. Before the guard hairs grow, the puppy coat is soft and far less water-resistant than the adult coat. Puppies should therefore be dried fully if they get caught in a shower. By the time they reach four to five months, they will have grown sufficient top coat to withstand most bad weather but it is still advisable to make sure they are dried soon after a wet walk. 'Oldies' appreciate a good towel-down too.

The Siberian's coat protects the dog in other ways. It acts as an insulator to keep a certain amount of heat and sunlight off the body. Basking in the sun or the heat from a fire is a favourite occupation for many Huskies and this can cause problems, since heat also has less opportunity to escape from the body than in shorter-coated breeds. You should be constantly aware of this if your dog is living in or enjoying warm and sunny conditions and ensure that he has shade and retires to it regularly. The Siberian copes well with heat due, in part, to his calm and relaxed nature and this, along with the nature of his coat, allows the dog to be comfortable in conditions that other breeds would find distressing. Providing a shady area, preferably with a breeze blowing

A Siberian's thick coat protects him from the cold and the wet, but it will take several months before a pup's coat is waterproof.

through, cold floor tiles or concrete, along with plenty of fresh water, will keep your Siberian happy throughout hot periods. Equally, it is essential to provide proper shelter for your dog to use in bad weather, although he will no doubt prefer to retire indoors with you!

GROOMING

The coat of the Siberian is fairly robust and does not need constant attention. However, there are times when nature can do with a hand. This may be as much to do with ensuring that the dog is pleasant to live with as with keeping the dog comfortable! The attention given by the owner during grooming, and the removal of dead, itchy coat, are certainly appreciated, providing you have accustomed your dog to this from early puppyhood.

Grooming is a way of interacting with your Siberian – as well as helping to remove loose hair.

Brushing and combing out the moulting coat can become a tedious task if not tackled routinely. Get both yourself and your dog into a regular routine at an early age so you can maintain a smart coat without unsightly woolly undercoat falling out. At the same time, this gives you the opportunity to check your dog over and assess his condition, checking his weight, ears, feet and so on, while noticing any minor cuts and scratches which would otherwise hide under that thick coat. Grooming ensures that you remain 'in touch' with your dog and it can strengthen your relationship.

GROOMING EQUIPMENT

The most suitable grooming materials for your dog will depend to a large extent on the texture and length of the coat. Most coat types respond well to the angled wire 'slicker'-type brushes but you should ensure that the one you choose is of good quality, with rounded tips to each wire to avoid scratching your dog's skin. A metal, wide-toothed comb is useful for cleaning out the brush and to tease through any coat tangles, particularly in the softer fur behind the ears and on the tail. Most dogs hate having their tails groomed but this is usually because the groomer is trying to hold it up to brush it. You will find that brushing the tail while your dog is lying down, and brushing only in the direction of the fur, will cause far less distress, since it avoids the tail being moved into an uncomfortable and unnatural position. A pair of round-ended scissors can be useful for trimming the hair around the feet but you will need very little else to keep your Siberian looking smart!

BATHING

Siberians do not need bathing too often; two or three times a year will usually be sufficient unless your dog is white and you show regularly! Bathing in warm water, using a dog shampoo, followed by thorough rinsing with a shower attachment, will leave your dog clean and sweet-smelling. During the summer months, your dog can be allowed to dry naturally in the garden but watch out for any loose earth or other interesting items which he may decide to roll in and ruin your hard work! In poor weather, you should towel him down and use a hair dryer if he will accept this. Once again, accustoming your dog to this while he is young is likely to reap dividends.

EXERCISE

Most Siberians walking on the lead will want to pull, as this natural instinct has been bred into him for generations. However, your Siberian can be taught to walk sensibly if you put in the effort: a course at the local Obedience class may be helpful. Choke chains are dangerous and pointless for trying to stop pulling but the harness-type or head collars can be effective once your dog becomes accustomed to one.

Regular daily exercise for the non-racing dog is essential. Those that exercise their Siberians in harness will develop their own exercise routine, which may well mean that some days the dogs are exercised while some days are for rest. Exercise for team dogs should continue all year round and, if the weather precludes summer-time training, then an early morning walk should replace running in harness. Year-round exercise is important for all dogs and Huskies are no exception: they are not motorbikes that can be switched off for the summer and switched back on when the racing season starts.

For dogs that are walked each day you should get into a routine that takes account of the weather, your lifestyle and the dog's age and fitness. A few tips may be helpful:

Who's walking whom? It is natural for Siberians to pull on the lead.

- Walks during the cooler part of the day in summer will reduce the possibility of heat stress.
- Half an hour to one hour every day of the week will be adequate for most Siberians, although most will enjoy more.
- Regular exercise will ensure a level of fitness that will then allow you to go for a three-hour hike at the weekend with no difficulty for either you or your dog.
- Adjust exercise levels for elderly dogs – give shorter walks.
- Puppies should be given limited exercise before they are fully grown; play and short walks are all that is required. Long walks should not be part of the puppy's routine while his bones are still growing.
- Ensuring that your dog cannot escape from either the house or the garden is essential, but his desire to

An extending lead will give your Siberian freedom, while you are still able to maintain control.

do so will be lessened if he receives regular exercise.

- Free-running is great for your Siberian if you can find a suitably fenced area.
- If not, then the use of an extending lead is invaluable. Your Siberian will quickly learn how far he can run before he gets to the end of the lead and he will slow down accordingly.

CARING FOR THE ELDERLY DOG
Siberian Huskies are a relatively long-lived breed and they usually remain healthy into their early teens, particularly if they have been kept fit and correctly fed.

You will probably find that your older dog needs a little more grooming and will benefit from a regular inspection by you. Run your hands over the body and legs to feel for any small lumps and bumps and, if any are found, get them looked at by the vet straight away. Checking teeth for tartar build-up and any breaks or discoloration is also important since these can lead to sore, uncomfortable gums.

Both food and exercise should be given 'little and often'. Maybe move to three small meals a day and a couple of short walks; you will be the best judge of what suits your oldie best. You may also find that food preferences will change and your dog will become more fussy. Most people find that giving whatever the dog likes best becomes a necessity as appetite diminishes. Relax your feeding rules: your dog's happiness in his older years is more important than following a perfect regime.

Older dogs generally appreciate a softer bed as they become stiffer and less agile. They may eventually need a helping hand with getting upstairs if that is where they normally sleep. If they become slightly incontinent, ensuring that they sleep on a suitably waterproof bed with a washable cover will lessen the inconvenience to you. No elderly dog should be chastised for such accidents – their house-training is still intact but they have simply lost full control, as often happens to elderly people. Ensuring that your dog gets frequent opportunities to go out will reduce the risk of accidents and keep him feeling happier too.

Some Siberians, particularly more senior pack members, become grumpier as they get older. Maintaining a senior position becomes harder and an aggressive stance may be the best way to cope with the situation from the dog's point of view. It helps if you are aware of this possibility and can help out.

Maintaining 'face' is what it is all about, so make sure that your oldies do not find themselves in the company of bullying, up-and-coming youngsters. Elderly dogs should be spending more time indoors away from the rest of the pack and you should supervise time spent together. Allowing oldies to think that they are still in charge, when you and the rest of the pack know differently, is all that matters in order to allow them to grow old gracefully.

An older dog will enjoy more of life's home comforts as he ages.

This is the time when, in general, your veterinary bill will start to increase. While Siberians are a healthy breed, you will nonetheless find that small and larger ailments start to develop more frequently. Get these problems treated early so that they do not have a chance to develop into a bigger and more expensive problem. Your elderly dog deserves all the care you can give him. Think back on all the years of friendship and love he has given you and you will know why you owe him every care as he gets older.

PACK MANAGEMENT

Suitable accommodation is as important for one Husky as it is for a pack, because to allow your dog to run loose or escape from a poorly secured run, house or garden is irresponsible and can cause harm both to your dog and to other animals. As Siberians are great excavators, suitable surfaces for runs include concrete, slabs or paving.

Concrete is easy to clean and can be disinfected regularly while, if well drained, it dries quickly. Treatment with suitable outdoor paint or resin finishes makes these surfaces particularly easy to clean and avoids the possibility of the run becoming smelly or unhygienic, which is particularly important if you are keeping a large pack. Concrete is ideal for cleaning but you should be aware that frost or ice can make the surface slippery, although the dogs will manage easily enough.

Stone or concrete slabs are also

suitable, although less hygienic since there are gaps between the slabs for dirt to lurk. Daily cleaning with a pressure hose and one of the modern multi-purpose disinfectants (not bleach) will ensure that the run remains smell- and germ-free. This, in turn, ensures that your dogs remain free from smell. The coat of the Siberian does not normally harbour odours, but lying around on urine-soaked concrete will certainly not help.

All your cleaning materials should be kept to hand in an area near the run and kennel. The essentials are: water supply, mop, bucket, hose, pet-specific disinfectant, shovel and faeces bucket. Plastic disposable gloves can also be helpful for messier tasks! The faeces bucket should have a fitting lid to ensure that flies are kept out and should be lined with plastic in order to maintain hygiene. Faeces disposal needs to be carried out in accordance with local laws: either sealed and placed in with your refuse, flushed down the outside drains or buried. Check with your local authority.

Concrete and slabs are obviously unyielding and, while these surfaces are suitable for dogs to lie on, they can lead to pressure sores, particularly on elbows. In any case, Huskies undoubtedly enjoy sitting and lying above ground. A slatted wooden platform allows air to circulate and will help to keep the dog cool and dry. You should ensure that the gaps between the slats are narrow

enough not to allow a foot to slip through and be caught between the supported planks. A wooden pallet or plastic barrel supported off the ground, provides a good sitting place and will be enjoyed by your Husky even if you do not have the space for a platform.

Suitable shelter from the rain and sun are a must if your dog is to spend time outside. It is worth noting that a constantly shaded area will be cooler than one that has to cool down once it becomes shady. A large parasol umbrella or pergola will provide shade if nothing more substantial is available. Your Siberian will shelter from the rain and sun when he wants to, but some dogs will sunbathe or stay out in the rain and you should use your judgement as to

Siberian Huskies are accomplished diggers.

when it may be necessary to bring them indoors. While the coat of the Siberian is very weather-resistant, the sun can cause skin damage and a thorough soaking from the rain will cause discomfort if nothing more.

HOUSING THE PACK

If you have a number of Siberians kept as a pack, you need to think out their living quarters carefully, particularly if your dogs do not come into the house. Siberians enjoy being part of the family, so coming indoors is a preferred option, but, if this is impossible, then you should spend time out with them. A dry and weatherproof living area which can be easily cleaned and is also suitable for humans to spend time in with the dogs, is ideal. Wooden platforms within the dog's indoor living area, will keep them off the ground and out of draughts, and will also prevent males from urinating on everyone else's bed! Oval plastic beds lined with 'fluffy' veterinary-type bedding are popular with most dogs and the bedding is easy to wash and dry. A kitchen for food preparation, washing and drying of bedding and storage of collars, leads and other equipment can prove highly convenient and time-saving.

CONTROLLING THE PACK

Packs require management. Putting a number of dogs in a run and leaving them to get on with it is a recipe for disaster. It is perfectly possible to feed

Shade must be provided in your dog's run.

10, 15 or even 20 dogs together and have them live harmoniously but only if you are in control and ensure that bad behaviour is not allowed. Routine is the key and is vital to successful management of large and small packs alike.

Preventing situations which could give rise to a fight in a pack situation is essential. The Siberian pack is hierarchical and an order will develop as each new dog arrives. This is more obvious in males through scent marking and aggressive physical posturing but females, too, have their hierarchy and any problems tend to be far more serious if they are allowed to develop between bitches. Posturing in males is most commonly displayed in eye-to-eye contact, and sudden changes to the social state can trigger actual fighting with resulting injuries. Injuries tend to

Siberians are great home-lovers.

be minor due to the Siberian's thick coat, but fighting should be avoided at all times. Dogs that appear to be normally calm with each other may be provoked by competition over food, for instance, and spark an attack. Bitches in season also provide an excuse!

It is important that the pack respects your authority. They need to be aware that fighting is totally unacceptable to you. This rule should be firmly established while the dogs are young and unable to cause much harm to each other.

PACK ROUTINE

A pack routine maintains a happy order and sense of security in the dogs. Feeding, cleaning and sleeping routines should remain mostly unchanged. Runs in harness, or walks on extending leads and lots of human company, are necessary parts of the daily routine. Visits from friends and passers-by are always welcome and add to the interest of the day. Climbing on platforms, playing in their run, chewing and guarding toys plus play-time with people and lots of 'cat naps' in between, keep dogs mentally stimulated. Any time you are going out and can take a dog or two with you for a special trip out, do so, even if it is just a quick visit to the shops with a stop in the park on the way home.

In the evening, time spent in the house, or watching TV in their own room (preferably with human company), or just lying in front of the fire makes a restful end to a busy day.

It requires a major commitment to give our dogs the best life we can, so, before you decide to increase your numbers, think carefully about the commitment required in terms of space, time and cost.

All this advice may sound like 'spoiling' but, once you have chosen to keep dogs, it will ensure that they are happy, well-adjusted companions. They will more than repay your efforts.

4 WORKING YOUR SIBERIAN

Because this most beautiful of breeds attracts so many people who have no interest in its working abilities, Siberians are often confined to the pet home and show ring. When you first acquire your Siberian Husky you may have no intention of working with him. This means that maintaining the Siberians' working characteristics and working attitudes, if they are not to be lost for ever in the years to come, requires dedication by those who are committed to working their dogs.

Many people, however, having initially been drawn to the Siberian by its beauty, discover that they also enjoy the working aspects of the breed, whether they live in cold or in relatively Mediterranean climates.

Racing is thrilling and exhilarating for both the dogs and the handlers. Iditarod 1997.

YOUR WORKING ADVENTURE

Before you start off on your working adventure you should ask yourself some fundamental questions. What is your aim, what do you want to achieve, what is your goal?

Your goal could be just to exercise your Siberian on a regular basis while enjoying all the pleasures of being outdoors – fresh air, early morning mists, sunrises and sunsets.

At the other extreme, your goal could be to establish a team of Siberians and race at the most competitive level possible at home or abroad.

In between these extremes is a full range of options and, indeed, your objectives may well change over time.

COLLECTING INFORMATION

Unless you understand those options and, perhaps, the commitment and rewards associated with them, you will be unable to make a decision.

So here is what you do. Contact a number of working kennels – any national Kennel Club will be able to put you in touch with them either directly or through the Breed Club – and make arrangements to go and visit. At this stage you will be taking notes and hitching lifts behind large teams in training, to get a sense of what is involved in running Siberians in harness.

You will, consequently, have made your first contact with dog drivers, sometimes called mushers (from the French 'marcher'), and these will be your source of learning how to work teams of Siberians.

This learning process, this acquisition of knowledge, is an ongoing, permanent feature of a driver's life. Hopefully, this information gathering will have started prior to your acquisition of Siberians, since it is always good to think that individuals will have work-in-harness as a core part of their Siberian's future, but that is not always the case.

MAKING COMPARISONS

It is important to visit a number of working owners. You need to view their different methods, their accommodation and their training venues, allowing you to make comparisons and build a picture of good practices, and establish exactly what will suit you as an individual.

Over the years we have found that advice, in the main, is freely acquired and freely given, openly, honestly and with a generosity of time, since drivers are proud of their Siberians, and what they have achieved. Most will give you ninety-eight per cent of what they have learnt over time. The additional two per cent is what they retain, that which, in competitive terms, gives them an advantage, or which will attract you back to learn that little bit more! It is that little bit extra, and you will learn it from your own experiences.

We are born with two ears and one mouth and the acquisition of knowledge is best pursued by using those senses in that proportion. Often, the best information is to be gleaned from the quietest individual. Watch and learn from the successful, bearing in mind that 'empty vessels can make the most noise'!

Another way in which to learn is to simply ask experienced drivers if you can help handle their dogs. By offering to help them, they will be keen to repay you by giving freely of help and advice.

Your decision to work your Siberians, and the exposure you have to 'riding shotgun' on other drivers' teams, will certainly help you understand the breed in the context of fit, form and function. The more years you ride behind working Siberians, the more you will understand structure and movement and, consequently, through this increased understanding, be able to breed better Siberians and build better sled dog teams.

Far too many drivers take the easy way out if a dog is not performing well and discard him in favour of a 'better' dog. It is much better to strive to realise each dog's full potential, both for their benefit and for yours as the driver.

BASIC RULES
There are some facts we must remember, facts that are irrefutable and that you will do well not to forget.

- A good Siberian will not reach physical maturity as an adult until he is at least three years old.
- A Siberian can run in harness from puppyhood through to 12+ years old; the years between 3 and 6-7

being the best in terms of performance.

- Remember that a Siberian thinks within a relatively simple framework. He wishes to please, and will perform in a manner which he thinks is right. Therefore, like it or not, Siberians do not make mistakes – drivers do. If a Siberian does not do what you expect him to do, it is because he does not know any better. He has not been trained satisfactorily to do things differently.
- Siberians are very sensitive to human mood swings, and they reflect their pack leader's mood in their performance. They know when they have done well and when things have not gone to plan. The performance of a team of Siberians will be positively or negatively influenced by the driver's mood. A feature of the most successful of teams is the wonderfully close relationship between driver and dogs, with the driver being super-sensitive to the individual dog's needs.
- There is a myth we must lay to rest. A good Siberian is a good Siberian. Siberians, by definition, can, and indeed should, given the proper training and conditioning, be able to carry a light load at a moderate speed over great distance. However, conditioning is what is important here and you can train Siberians to participate in sprint racing and then, in a season, those same Siberians can

45

be conditioned to participate in long-distance races. These Siberians are not different – they are merely prepared and conditioned in a different way to achieve different objectives.

- Each and every time you run your team of dogs, you will have a new learning experience, both you and your dogs. It is never the same experience and so it allows you to build up your knowledge base. As you leave the start, following 'hook-up', be ready and equipped for any eventuality – even after years of experience you will be faced with new situations on a regular basis!

FUNDAMENTAL ATTRIBUTES

A good working Siberian must possess four fundamental attributes if he is to enjoy a long working life. We emphasise long, since these attributes are not only important in the context of the competitive aspect of today's working Siberian, but in good measure they will allow the Siberian to maximise working potential, since they describe the standard Siberian.

1. A GOOD 'HEAD'

This is not a cosmetic requirement alone, although physical features of the head are important to maintain breed type and to cope with adverse weather conditions. In this context we refer to the concept of working attitude, mental

A study in mental toughness: Ditko of Sepp-alta. Courtesy: Simon Dainty.

toughness, focus and concentration on the work in hand.

A Siberian who has not the desire to run is not a Siberian. Working attitude is a critically important feature of this wonderful breed, and dogs who lack this quality are better excluded from your breeding programme.

Siberians tend to possess working attitude in different measure; at one end of the scale there is a tendency towards some indifference, at the other end of the scale is total obsession.

Certain lines of dogs, can be described as 'hyper' or verging on a state of mind which is out of control when it comes to 'hook-up'. At this extreme, it could be argued that this is not typically 'Siberian'. The ideal is the Siberian who clearly differentiates his work from his day-to-day routine, who is prepared to give his driver his full attention, concentration and hard physical effort throughout the work activity, and who, despite a myriad of counter-attractions, will remain absolutely focused while in harness.

It is said that a Siberian will 'work till it drops'. That is not actually true of the pure-bred Siberian Husky, who will always keep a little in reserve, believing that he will have to provide the same effort the following day. That does not mean he is not working his heart out for you; it means he has the intelligence to balance his effort throughout the duration of the activity for which he has been conditioned, and can complete that task to the best of his ability, without actually doing himself any permanent physical damage.

Mental toughness is both real and observable. When driving dogs in adverse weather conditions; on trails that become poor; when you have a distracting incident; when a dog takes a tumble: these are examples of situations when a tough dog will stand out within a team.

A mentally tough dog will cope with all sorts of adversity and will apparently work even harder for you. When you observe the team from behind, while other dogs are showing signs of sensitivity or distraction, looking around and with a little inconsistency in the tug line, the tough dog will 'tuck and drive' with a tight tug line, head absolutely still, focused on the trail ahead, with a top line that could carry a glass of champagne without spilling a drop, driving, driving

and listening to your words.

Working attitude combined with the mental toughness exhibited by exceptional Siberians will, when harnessed to the natural willingness to please, provide you with the 'good head' you seek.

2. EATING AND DRINKING WELL!

There is nothing worse than a fussy eater! From puppyhood onwards you can tell the voracious eaters in your household, and a dog that has a healthy appetite and drinks well is a blessing.

Appreciation of the good eater only comes when faced with the alternative. Dogs that pick at their food, leave some, will not eat 'on the road', and will not drink either during water stops in training or in the run-up to competition, are quite a burden.

Accepting that you are providing a quality diet to fit the occasion, the timing of feeding and watering is an important factor in undertaking the conditioning process, and subsequently competing on the trail.

Water, as will be mentioned on more than one occasion, is critical to the overall wellbeing of your Siberian, and a regular intake of good water will avoid dehydration and aid in recovery.

Eating and drinking 'on the road', or away from home, is something that may well have to be practised in the travelling vehicle at home, before away trips are undertaken. Rather like a puppy that will try and resist 'nature's call' when not on his home ground, travelling is, initially, more than likely to affect the desire of youngsters to eat properly. So feeding your Siberians in your vehicle at home, which will at least give them the experience of some normality, may help counter the wide variety of different distractions on offer while they are away.

3. ATHLETICISM

The Breed Standard, described elsewhere in this book, refers to a smooth and effortless gait, "quick and light on feet", with "good reach and good drive". So it will come as no surprise that another key attribute is athleticism. To combine power, speed and endurance effectively you must have a Siberian with excellent balance throughout. There will be times during work that a Siberian will have to run at a constantly fast speed for a period of time, before breaking off into an extended trot as the team drives hard up a hill. Adjusting to these changing requirements with an economy of effort, while producing optimum performance, will require a first-class athletic performance. Any structural defects will become apparent over the conditioning for distance should the dog not possess all the necessary physical attributes.

4. FEET

The fourth important attribute for the top-class Siberian is good feet. So what do we mean by good feet? The key to

Raring to go: Siberians should combine power, athleticism, and endurance.

this lies again in reference to the Standard. "Oval", rather than small and round in shape. A good-sized foot in proportion to the dog, in shape and appearance often referred to as a "modified hare-foot", with pads "tough and thickly cushioned", is vital.

You can have all the attributes of a perfect Siberian, but if he is cursed with poor feet, the dog and you are going to struggle through a working life of bootees, potions, ointments and some discomfort to the Siberian.

A well-cushioned, well-knuckled-up foot, with tough pads, is a work of art. Over the years, those Siberians with 'lemon' pads and with good strong nails, capable of taking plenty of wear, have proved to us to be even tougher than the black, fully pigmented pads. In any event, some dogs possess thinner pads than may be at first obvious. For this reason, your dogs' feet should be checked each and every time they are in harness.

EATING AND DRINKING

Nutrition and the Siberian Husky is the subject of a separate section; however, there are a number of points worth raising here which are working-specific.

Control over the quality and quantity of food is most important when working, and especially when racing your Siberian. If you do not know for sure how much or what you are feeding your dog, you are effectively in an out-of-control situation.

David Nicholson known as 'the Duke' and one of the UK's greatest National Hunt racehorse trainers, commented when asked about food that "a top-quality food and plenty of hard work" is the key to success. In this day and age there is a temptation to play with additives to enhance performance in harness. But, by comparison to even ten years ago, the all-in-one foods have been developed to a level of sophistication that requires no addition. Indeed, additives will tend to unbalance a balanced content.

If you feed meat, be sure that you know what is in it; be comfortable with the quality. Many people we know grind their own food to guarantee the content. The main point is that a Siberian is a relatively small dog and guessing by handful, rather than specifically weighing, or using measures of some other type like cups, may result in over or underfeeding.

Feeding twice rather than once a day will help the digestive process – little and often rather than in one lump. Prior to working, it is important that the last meal has passed through the system, and, particularly on a single race day, make sure that the last full meal was consumed around eighteen hours beforehand.

On normal training days, adult dogs will not have been fed within the previous 12 hours. Puppies may well have been fed, but just a little and often, and anyway puppy training runs are somewhat different to hard conditioning activity on a partly-full stomach.

Water, as we have said, is most important and should be readily available. A 40lb dog requires two pints of water a day at least. Under the headings of training and racing we refer

Water stops during training are vital.

to the practice of watering during training, and watering prior to competition, both essential practices which are important preventatives against dehydration.

Following the training/conditioning activity it is good to have a special reward – a reward that the dogs relate to working hard in harness. We use liver, which can be frozen and given in a semi-frozen condition. Liver is the 'magic' food and brings much to the diet of your Siberians. The dogs love it and two one-inch cubes will be much appreciated when they have had a drink and are cooling off following their exercise.

An alternative to liver cubes could be warm dog soup, which can be equally acceptable. Two cups of meat-based broth has the advantage of encouraging dogs to reintroduce fluids into their systems during the recovery phase but care must be taken not to 'over do' the soup, as some dogs will not be able to keep it down.

Once recovery has taken place, the dogs may have one of their two daily meals around two hours after working. Ideally, the second meal will be fed around six to eight hours after the first.

Feeding regimes for long-distance conditioning and racing are somewhat different and rely on steady work, rest and regular food intake over a period of days, with routine playing an important part.

After working, it is important to 'drop' your dogs to answer nature's

call within one to two hours. If you have been watering during training and following a good take-up of water at the end of exercise, the fluids will pass quickly through the system and the dogs will be anxious to relieve themselves.

Monitoring dogs' stools and urine is, of course, an excellent way to assess a dog's general health and level of hydration.

EQUIPMENT

The quality and condition of your equipment will have a significant impact on your working activity. Equipment falls broadly into the following areas: harnesses and lines, vehicles, and other items.

HARNESSES

There are two types of harness style – cross-back or H-back. Both have their supporters and both have been used for many years on the trail. With two such proven styles, other aspects become important, in particular the fit of the harness.

The harness should be made of a soft, flexible webbing type of material, which is easily washable, but also retains its shape over time. Inflexible, rigid or stiff material, which can cut into the dog and quickly shrink or stretch out of shape, should be avoided at all costs. In recent years, the leading equipment suppliers have adopted a parachute-type of webbing, with either a waterproof or fleece pad around the shoulders,

An H-back harness.

A cross-back harness.

which provides comfort when the dogs are pulling.

The important areas of fit for the harness are around the neck, rib cage and croup. The neck fitting should be fairly tight yet comfortable. When fitted, you should just be able to insert two fingers between the dog's neck and the harness.

The major equipment suppliers colour-code harnesses according to the size of the dog and, therefore, it is likely with a standard-size Siberian, if you get the correct neck size, you will also have the appropriate overall body fitting. You will, however, have a choice of length for the tug loop running off the dog's croup.

The snap, usually made of a good-quality brass, and the attachment between the tug line and harness, should hook to the harness loop about three inches behind the dog's croup. Adjusting the final length of the harness loop is best done when the lines are laid out on the ground; harnesses are

attached to the snap, with measurements taken from the front of the harness to the neckline.

One of the most common errors made by new drivers is that, through incorrect measurements and poor fitting, the dog ends up not pulling on his tug line, but pulling on his neckline. This is usually because the neckline is positioned parallel to, or backward of, the dog's neck on the gangline, instead of slightly forward, and in line with the dog's muzzle.

LINES

Again, these need to be light, flexible, easily washable and well maintained. If at any time there are signs of wear and tear, and this also applies to snaps and harnesses, they must be replaced. This is not an area in which to compromise and, ultimately, the safety of your dogs and yourself depends on your diligence.

Polypropylene is the most often-used material in line making, and this is easily obtainable either locally in major cities,

51

or it may be purchased in spools from major North American equipment suppliers, who will also export a wide range of other items on request.

The make-up and measurement of your lines is crucial. Not only must the line be strong, tough and flexible, but the measurement of gang, tug and necklines must be accurate, and must fit with your harness, and the make-up should ensure that measurements are consistent throughout, with no chance of line failure or separation. Connecting the lines to the harnesses will normally be some style of snap. Most commonly used is a high-quality brass trigger snap. Again, this should be regularly checked for signs of wear, and a regular wash or rinse of all lines and snaps will ensure that foreign matter will not foul the spring mechanism of the snap.

Some dogs, particularly youngsters, may resort to line-biting, which is biting or chewing the line during hook-up. Teaching the dog that this is unacceptable behaviour is one way of resolving this problem, but inserting a cable, probably of coated wire, through your training lines will reduce the risk of your team separating, and consequential dog injury.

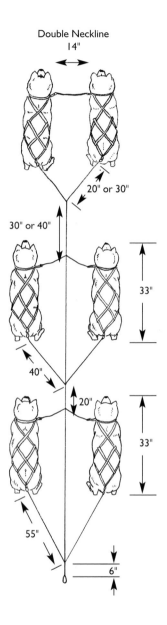

TRAINING/RACING PLATFORMS

Sleds are of course the 'normal' platform for working, training and racing, where weather and conditions permit. Sleds are, in the main, made from wood, although other materials have been tested over time, from light metals to composites.

One of the most commonly used woods is white ash, which combines flexibility and toughness, and is relatively light. Other harder, heavier woods include hickory, which is often used for training sleds, and is well capable of taking the knocks associated with day-to-day use.

For the driver/musher, a sled is a very personal thing, with the preference for style, and the 'feel' of it being developed over time. Drivers will take time to select a sled, but may then keep that sled for years, refurbishing it as wear takes its toll.

Selecting and acquiring sleds is best done in a country where there is a variety available from well-established sled builders. Buying a sled at a distance can be fraught with difficulty. Since it could be a lifetime's investment, take the time and trouble to travel if necessary to make a good purchase.

ATVs

Today, most dirt training for larger groups of dogs is undertaken using 'Quads', also known as All Terrain Vehicles (ATVs). These are readily available new or second-hand, and provide ideal control of a team – provided, of course, you do not hook up too many dogs to too small an ATV!

Some choose to train their dogs using an ATV chassis frame, having removed the engine. This is an excellent chassis platform, and of course reduces the weight and removes any of the engine noise distraction.

Prior to the use of ATVs, all sorts of home-made vehicles were put together to train dogs – everything from simple, chariot-type welded frames made from car or bicycle components, to car chassis. The problem facing these structures, as opposed to ATVs, was that they frequently needed repairing after use over rough ground since they tended not to have suspension.

For smaller teams, or single-dog training, the trainer can use bicycles, or, of course, skis on snow. While sounding straightforward, it requires no little skill to achieve!

DIRT TRAINING

Running on dirt, an activity which has become increasingly popular over the last twenty years in snowless terrain, has resulted in the development of highly sophisticated race rigs, originally based on bicycle components but now using more exotic materials and manufactured to bespoke designs, either by the driver for himself, or on a made-to-order basis. No little skill is involved in this activity,

A selection of training vehicles.

and potential buyers should spend time studying different styles.

It is difficult to generalise as to the weight and size of your dirt training platform. So much depends on the terrain on which you train. Is it flat or hilly; is the surface firm, soft or sandy? Do you want to carry passengers? How much do you want to invest? The advice would be to remain flexible. It may be necessary to have two, or even three, vehicles if you have a group of dogs in training.

LIGHTING

One other aspect that you should not forget is lighting. Depending on your commitments you may choose to train your dogs in the dark. In such circumstances it is most important that you have excellent lighting. Powerful

A lot of training takes place in the early hours, so adequate lighting is essential. Photo: Stu Forster.

halogen lamps can easily be run off long-life batteries. Dog teams get a thrill from running in the dark chasing shadows, and running speeds often seem, and in fact may actually be, faster. In those circumstances if you have any problems, such as a tangle, it is important that your lighting allows you to see it quickly.

OTHER ESSENTIAL ITEMS

There are other items which form an important part of the driver's equipment, each of which could be discussed in some detail but probably only warrant a line here.

- A shock-absorption system within the lines which allows the dogs to lunge forward without jarring their spinal columns. Most often contained within the gangline behind the wheel dogs, it can also be in the individual tug lines, or even as a part of the rear of the harness.
- A snow or dirt hook which will allow you to hold the team when you want to stop and attend to the dogs. In addition to this, you need a snub line which attaches to the rearmost part of the team's ganglines and will allow you safe anchorage when you stop and attach the snub line to a post or tree. This is also the device you use, the quick-release clip on the snub line, to release your team when you have completed hook-up at the start and are ready to go. It is important

Fleece boots help dogs to cope with difficult surfaces.

that the snub line is attached directly to the team.

- A dog-bag should be available to allow you to carry a tired dog back to the finish in comfort. This bag should be functional and ready for use, not merely a cosmetic item.

- Dog bootees should always be available no matter how many dogs you are running. A range of things can cause a dog to bruise or have a sore foot. A comfortable fleece bootee with a Velcro attachment will resolve the problem quickly, and may allow you to continue.

- We always carry a knife, and a double clip for emergencies. There are rare occurrences when you have a complex tangle which may result in half the team of dogs continuing to tug and pull on a tangled dog's neck or leg, and it proves quite impossible to release the dog. A knife can quickly cut a line to release the dog, thus preventing the risk of stress and serious injury. A double clip – a double brass trigger snap – has many uses. Most typically they can be used to quickly replace failed snaps, out on the trail. It is always handy to have one on your belt or in your pocket.

- Two final comments about lines. Typically these will be attached to your sled/rig/ATV by a karabiner, or looped directly into a suitable attachment point on the platform. It is critical that your lines are set at the right height in relation to the ground and the back of your team – neither too high, which could prevent a dog escaping a tangle, or too low to the ground, which will result in dogs constantly crossing lines during running. Dogs should be able to pull on a level plane when leaning into the harness.

- Laying out your lines in front of your vehicle will allow you a final, not first, check that all is well prior to hook-up. Check each snap and each line joint for signs of wear. You cannot be too careful.

TRANSPORT

There seem to be as many types of vehicles and vehicle arrangements for transporting sled dogs as there are sled dogs running in harness.

You have a choice of either a bespoke vehicle, or a trailer, or some modification to your normal day-to-day vehicle. Focusing on trucks and vans and trailers, there are some quite simple rules.

- Dogs need to travel in comfort. The space provided must not be too much, nor too little; there must be room for movement but it must also be snug for comfort. Cleanliness is vital and there is also the matter of companionship with a travelling friend. Dogs like to travel with their particular friends. We all know that they develop preferences over time, and if they travel in comfort with a friend they will relax and stress will be minimal.

- Good ventilation is important.
- Quick and easy double access, from the front and the back of a transporter or cage, in the event of an accident.
- The box or cage surface on which the dogs stand should be non-slip, and the boxes themselves must be as quiet and noise-free as possible, and easy to clean out.
- Puppies may find initially that travelling induces motion sickness. Although there are many home remedies for this, the short answer is that 99 per cent will grow out of it.
- When travelling to a training site or a race, allow plenty of time, get there early, relax the dogs, stay overnight before a race if necessary, and, on the way, stop regularly to allow the dogs to meet the calls of nature.

TRAINING AND CONDITIONING
Training is a process of education and learning. The majority of training, the critical base-training, takes place in the formative years. But, as with humans, the learning or training process lasts, to some degree, for a lifetime.

Conditioning, however, is something different – it concerns fitness. While training, conditioning can also be achieved; while you learn, at the same time you can achieve a degree of conditioning. When you are training and educating your dogs you are also conditioning them. As your dogs grow older, so the emphasis moves towards conditioning, and conditioning yearlings is very different to conditioning older dogs.

A fundamental requirement of training your dogs is that you are able to exercise control at all times. This will create a bond of confidence between you and your dogs. The dogs will quickly learn that you are in control of the team, and you and your dogs will have the confidence to be able to manage any situation that may arise.

The critical aspects of control involve your ability to be able to brake, stop and hold the team at your command; this capability is, of course, greatly enhanced with fully-operational equipment. To limit the potential for failure, checking and cleaning your equipment on a frequent basis is critical.

One aspect that is frequently ignored is the ability to translate experience, skills and knowledge acquired from other situations, to help in the training of sled dogs. Therefore if you possess knowledge and skill from, say,

Correct training and conditioning makes record-breakers. Pictured: Tom Iliffe (Towman kennels, Canada) setting a record for the Bancroft Trail in 1998 – just over four miles in 13 minutes 59 seconds.

performing at a top level in another sport, much of this can prove useful in training sled dogs.

While this is not always the case, training should be a fun, positive experience. Sled dogs with attitude love to run – they will enjoy it if you enjoy it. As mentioned earlier, sled dogs can pick up your mood very quickly. If you are low or down, then your dogs will be the same; dogs can quickly pick up your disappointment, and will be negatively affected by it.

KEEPING RECORDS

To assist you in your management of training and conditioning it is important to keep accurate records. Venues, dates, temperatures, humidity, who runs where on the team, distances, training vehicles used, additional comments – which will include how certain dogs perform, bitches in season, and observations you may have. These will form a critical part of your knowledge database, as well as being fun and interesting to look back on in years to come.

TRAINING PERIODS

There is no reason why, climate permitting, you cannot run your sled dogs all the year round. Much depends on your level of interest, and commitment. In the UK during the summer months, from four o'clock to six o'clock in the morning, when the temperatures are below 15 degrees C, are great opportunities for hook-ups.

During those summer months when you are engaged purely in fun runs eight to ten times a month, this will maintain basic conditioning in your dogs. During the winter, up to 16 times a month will allow you to build that base into hard conditioning. We find fifteen to sixteen hook-ups per month are about right; more, and you will risk sourness after a period of time.

Top canine athletes are like top human athletes. They always like and need to undertake a level of exercise to retain fitness. If all activity ceases for a period of time, and consequently fitness is lost, there is a risk, certainly as dogs mature, that they may never regain their peak levels of fitness.

If we accept the premise that we gain reward and satisfaction from doing any activity well, so it is with sled dog training. Dogs will learn from positive experiences, quality training and conditioning. Negative experiences such as allowing dogs to take wrong turns, or putting them in a position where they cannot achieve that which you are asking them to do due to lack of fitness, is the road to disaster.

Canine athletes need year-round training to maintain fitness levels.

PUPPY TRAINING

Pups can start training from as young as 18 weeks. Much depends on your level of knowledge and your preferences. Some will prefer not to start puppy training until six months or even older.

Remember puppies are physically very vulnerable at this age, and psychologically they are learning about the world around them. So there are both physical and mental aspects you have to manage for them through good decision-making. Bad experiences, like a knock, or tumble, or a tangle, or being expected to run too fast, may be something a youngster will not forget easily. Thus control, absolute confidence in what you are doing, and, possibly, some outside help, are important. It is far better to wait until dogs are older and probably more able to cope, than to start too young.

New pups can first be walked in harness on their own to experience the new feel of the harness on the body. Then they can run with others in front of a rig or bicycle. Walking a puppy in harness, with the lead on the harness loop, is easily managed. When walking in harness, however, it is best that the puppy is discouraged from sniffing or loafing about. This can be achieved by following some bait – either an older dog or a partner or friend walking out in front at a distance. For pulling in harness there is always reward at the finish, some type of favourite treat.

It is important that Huskies learn to pull. To most this will come naturally, others will need monitoring. If they do not learn to pull, they may just learn to 'run along'. This is a habit that can be acquired when you run puppies too fast with adult dogs, that is dogs that are running beyond the puppies' 'pulling speed'.

Puppies approaching six months of age can be attached in harness on lines in front of a bicycle. If a single puppy has a friend or companion, excitement and competition usually sweep away any doubt over pulling forward. If any hesitation exists, the bait of a family member running out of sight around a corner is usually more than enough to start the chase, combined with lots of encouragement and possibly a little help by pedalling or pushing the training vehicle.

This first experience is difficult for new Siberians, and new owners alike. It is very delicate, in fact, since there is much that can go wrong.

These first outings must, of course, be taken on a good trail surface, and over a short distance – say half a mile. Introducing puppies to running with the help of other Siberian adults is, by comparison, easy. It is important to ensure that pups are run next to tolerant, but no-nonsense adults from whom they will learn good practices about pulling and working generally, and not bad habits like line-biting.

A puppy's reaction to his first experience in harness will vary. Some will, from day one, run in a focused, head-down, fully concentrated manner. Others will be all over the place, looking at their surroundings, trying to play with their teammates, paying more attention to wildlife than to the task in hand. Firmness matched with tolerance is important at this stage. In these early runs, most of your comments will be directed towards encouraging the newcomer.

This new experience of work will be easy for the pups if they can be introduced to it via a team of oldies or veterans. Often kennels will allow you to introduce your Siberian to working in this way by running in a friend's team. But beware! The puppy may not know the other dogs, and may not recognise the driver's voice, so there are a lot of issues to consider.

Another important introduction for pups can be to take them along to watch teams of dogs in training. They can see dogs at hook-up and return. They can become acquainted with the noise and atmosphere.

Many books talk about puppies pulling tyres as an early learning experience. We have no real view on this technique, except to mention it here. It is something we have no experience of, and have found it unnecessary in the training of our dogs.

BALANCING TEAMS
Selecting your teams for running is important. In the first instance the dogs should be rotated side to side, and from front to back, in order to develop a balanced physique and muscling from running in different positions. They should also learn to run with different partners, to give you that flexibility for team selection. In the same way as we are right- or left-handed, dogs inevitably will have a preference about which side they prefer to run.

They will also have, in some cases, greater aptitude to run in lead, swing/point, team or wheel. But you must develop the individual dog's potential to the full and establish just what that dog's capability is.

Where possible, the team should be of balanced or equal ability. High performers will be frustrated or blunted by low or non-performers. Remember, to achieve quality work for the youngest, or slowest, or oldest member of your selected team, whichever is the limiting factor, you have to run at the speed of that dog. Faster dogs will be pulling even harder, but unable to go at the speed they want. If you run at their speed, the slower dog will be run off his feet and not pulling.

Select your teams before training, then make out your written team sheet which should view your team from the driver's position, with the leaders at the top of the page and the wheelers at the bottom, or closest to you. Display the sheet in a prominent place during hook-up, usually on the side window of the truck. Plan your training meticulously before you set out. Know the trail, the distance, the temperature, the team, your training vehicle, and just exactly what it is you are setting out to achieve. Have a fall-back position just in case. How many times have we all set off only to find we are unable to access our intended venue!

When selecting the size of your team for training, to repeat what we have stated earlier, control is everything. Therefore balancing the size of the team with the inclusion of veterans with young pups, and fast with slow dogs, becomes a task in itself.

Veterans require particular conditioning to continue their racing careers. Pictured: Zima Tekla, aged 11 years.

When you have dogs of different capabilities, it is well worthwhile running two groups, and is more considerate to the dogs.

THE OLDER DOG
As dogs age they require a different level and type of conditioning. Accepting that optimum performance is from around two and a half years old to six years old, conditioning the veteran (seven-plus years) is an art. Pups and yearlings require special attention, but you can also have the wise or clever veteran who gives all the appearances of working and pulling hard, but is actually only keeping the tug line taut while putting limited weight on it.

Large dogs can require a different approach to training than light dogs. A

55lb male is somewhat different from a 35lb bitch. Awareness of these differences is so important. The training techniques do not change, but their application can vary from dog to dog.

TRAINING DISTANCE AND SPEED
Siberians like to lope when training. Some have the ability to perform an extended trot, and indeed this can be as fast as some other Siberians lope, but that is the exception. Therefore, Siberians will lope as far as their fitness and the trail conditions allow. That is, of course, unless the team has been specifically trained for long-distance races, where drivers frequently condition for fast trotting over great distances.

Siberians will set off on their training run at a fast lope, settling into a comfortable rhythm after a mile or so. This then will be their pace for as long as fitness allows. When they come off the lope, it is an opportunity for you to rest your team. Remember, we are looking for quality conditioning. The dogs want to lope, as much as you want them to, so by stopping on these occasions, they will realise the consequence of their ceasing to lope is that you will stop the team. Impact: they will in future lope even further, not wishing to stop. If you do not stop, the team will think trotting is acceptable and you will develop aspects of good and bad training in your hook-ups.

If you start at a level where your team can lope the full distance from say two miles for adults (half a mile upwards for pups) and steadily increase in increments of a half a mile every seven to ten outings, you will, with a limited size team of eight dogs or less, quickly develop a team that can run at a lope a distance which can be roughly calculated at up to a mile and a half per team member. So three miles for two dogs, six to eight miles for six dogs. This is on flat trails and merely a guide. The regular repetition and incremental increases comprise, however, the important activity in achieving fitness and hard conditioning.

There are differences between conditioning on snow and dirt. Variations in dirt conditions are arguably far more limited than in snow. Dirt is either wet or dry, or frozen, and the consequential rolling resistance, or drag, will be only marginally different.

Snow can be manicured to a slick, no-resistance surface, or, at the other extreme, can be wet, heavy and melting. In these circumstances, the same distance will provide two entirely different results. Perhaps another way to make a comparison is that fast, firm, rolled dirt and grass is somewhat similar to 'manicured' snow, while a wheeled vehicle moving through sand is not unlike running a sled through heavy, wet snow.

The distances you train and condition will all be geared towards some goal you have. This may or may not be competitive races. If it is, the

A working Siberian is a happy Siberian.

conditioning programme should be complete at least two weeks before the race date, so that the dogs can rest a little after this hard preparation. Believe it or not, rest has a very important part to play in the conditioning of your dogs!

There are different types of conditioning and you will have to include all aspects during your team's build-up. Heavy training is rather akin to the weight training an athlete does in the gym. It is most important to build the muscle base on which the race conditioning can be built. In a way, it stretches the dog to the extremes of his potential. Pulling significant weights over medium distance will be the hardest you will ever require the dog to work.

Light, or speed, conditioning is in some way a simulation of competition where dogs are pulling lighter loads, and are encouraged to increase the average speed by 25 per cent.

Too much heavy training will result in muscle-bound dogs. Too much speed training will result in dogs which are lacking muscle and physical condition. It is a delicate balance.

In both scenarios, you can undertake interval training. Human athletes will run around an athletic track, jogging 200 metres and sprinting 200 metres alternately. The same principle can be applied to Siberians, not by loping and trotting, but by use of the training vehicle brake and through voice commands.

Using half-mile intervals, you can teach your Siberians to pick up on command, driving extra-hard for periods, before resting them at the slower lope.

TRAINING PATTERNS
There are many patterns and preferences – day on/day off, two on/one off, three on/two off etc. Again, there are so many influences that will determine the pattern. Remember though, in hard training, 16 outings a month is as much as dogs need, and do mix serious work with the occasional purely fun outing. We would certainly suggest two days off following two days of stressful competition, followed by a fun hook-up to get back into the work routine.

It is thought that a three-day gap will cost you a day's conditioning but this is doubtful, particularly if the three-day gap is, say, once a month. Indeed, a fit dog could probably miss a week without significant ill effects, and catch up in a run or two.

Measuring fitness levels is difficult, but one way, which is probably as good as any, is simply to observe the speed of recovery following a period of intense physical activity. We can all tell the difference between dogs that have found an activity relatively easy and those who have found it tough. Fit dogs will recover quickly and, an hour or so after activity, will show no apparent signs of strain or stress.

DEVELOPING A UNIT

It is a popular myth that you should run your lightweight bitches at the front of your team and your strong males on wheel.

Perhaps we should first identify the team's positions. Your lead dogs are at the front, and behind your leaders you have your 'point' or 'swing' dogs. Swing is the name given to this position in the team in Alaska. Outside Alaska this position in the team is frequently referred to as point. All other dogs,

apart from those immediately in front of your rig or sled which are referred to as wheel dogs, are known as team dogs.

The dog's athleticism, aptitude and your need will ultimately determine where a dog runs in a team. Some of the larger male Siberians can also be the most athletic and possess the greatest drive and speed. Why would you not train these to run in front? Some of the lighter Siberians may not have the confidence to run in front, and will be happier at swing. It is dangerous to generalise.

However, it is true to say that your 'wheelers' will receive a fair amount of pushing about from the gangline when cornering and, of course, will have the close vicinity of the rig or sled to cope with.

It is important to give your dogs every opportunity to develop as balanced animals and, as we have said before, through rotation try them in every position on the team. How often is it said, "he always runs on the right wheel because he likes it"? Well, how do you

Careful thought must go into choosing the dogs' positions in the team.

know that is true if he has been developed as a one-sided sled dog, with no opportunity elsewhere in the team!

It is worth considering the issue of bitches in season at this point. Depending on the degree of sensitivity of your bitches to their season, you should consider your lead dog options. Bitches who follow a six-month cycle can be less than 100 per cent for 6 months of the year. That said, some exceptional bitches are not apparently affected by their seasons, and will drive your team hard all the year round. These bitches are super to have, particularly if they are of a good size and mentally tough.

When selecting your team, speed and athleticism will dictate your final decision, but, yes, you are likely to have some medium to large Siberians on wheel, and, yes, some fast, hard drivers in front. Apart from the enjoyment of the dogs and their wanting to run with their chosen partner (and some do enjoy particular team-mates more than others) that is as much as you can say.

Having identified a team for competitive purposes, much can be gained from developing that team as a unit. We are always fascinated by the way some drivers chop and change their team. In the same way that you can optimise an individual dog's capabilities, so too you can really develop teamwork. A really good team will always gain the upper hand over a group of talented but disparate individuals.

Dogs enjoy training in the dark. Pictured: Ch. Zima Toaki and Zima Wapahkwa. Photo: Stu Forster.

COMMAND TRAINING

Training dogs to run in front, assuming responsibility for both the speed of the team and the direction, is one of the most rewarding aspects of running sled dogs.

There are four fundamental commands: a right turn is "Gee", left turn is "Haw", "Go on" is to keep straight on at, say, a crossroads or remain on a trail where a turn-off is an option, and "Wooah" for slow and stop. In addition you can call "Get up" to pick up the pace, and "Steady" for a downhill or braking manoeuvre, where you want them to listen carefully and slow a little.

Drivers will have their own commands as variants, but the key is consistency of command and also consistency of voice. If dogs are trained by a whole variety of different people, who call commands differently, at different times relative to the turn for example, then confusion will occur. And remember, it is not the dog's fault!

A consistent voice command, and necessary encouragement, is all that is needed. If a dog needs a reprimand then a sharp call will suffice, but unnecessary chitchat for the length of the trail will only cause the dogs to switch off.

Training pups from the start is tough and requires understanding, care and patience. Nevertheless, take time, do not allow them to make mistakes and get away with it, since they will confuse commands.

Very simply, young pups will learn best on a simple trail with a few turns, through repetition and encouragement. So a trail of say two miles with five or six turns is ideal to practise commands. This trail should be run repeatedly until not only are the youngsters running the trail 'in their sleep' but, as they reach a turn, they associate the directional change with a particular command. This reinforcement through repetition will result in the average puppies picking up commands quite quickly.

With your first run, and with all subsequent runs for training, when you come to a turn, call a command and, if the leaders do not take it, stop and hold the team until the leaders revise their selection and correct their mistake because, as we have said before, you do at all times retain control! A fundamental mistake many drivers make is to allow their 'front end' to make a mistake and get away with it without correction – you are doing yourself and the team a disservice.

Trained lead dogs do not have to receive further experience during conditioning. Once trained, a Siberian will not forget how to run in front, or the commands. Training should be used to, as it implies, train other Siberians to run in lead.

If you have experienced lead dogs, then they can act as perfect tutors to train youngsters to run in front. Some are better tutors than others; some have great confidence, but may not be able to take on the tutor role without making errors themselves.

Some Siberians have the potential to be natural leaders from the earliest age and will drive head-down in a focused manner, constantly listening to the driver and responding to commands quickly and accurately. Other, slower learners may take months, even a year or so, to develop into reliable leaders. That said, these slow learners can also be the most reliable, and a greater long-term investment for you.

If you take the time and the trouble, you can train 99 per cent of all Siberians to run lead. Whether or not you want them there, or they want to be there, is a different matter. But remember – flexibility.

PASSING PRACTICE
A team that is capable of coping with unexpected events during work is far easier to control. 'Unexpected events' will include people, animals, fallen trees and a myriad of other possibilities. It may also include other teams, particularly if you train in an area with

others. Training your team to pass others without interference will therefore assist you not only in competition but also in other situations.

The simplest training can be provided by working with friends who have other teams. Starting off at intervals, the lead team will allow the following team to catch up by braking. When the follower is ready to overtake, they will call 'trail', the leader moving to one side of the trail to allow clear passage. As the follower pulls parallel the leader will brake to allow the follower to accelerate through quickly.

The follower during this procedure will encourage the team to "Get up", that is, to pick up the speed, and if any team members move towards the team being overtaken, a sharp reprimand of "Leave" should make for a clear passing movement.

This passing procedure may be practised several times during a training run to reinforce the experience. It should not be long before the team will pass with almost total disregard for others.

Head-on passing is best practised on a wide trail, using at least one experienced team. Two young puppy teams will quite often end up tied in a knot, which is a very negative experience. The oncoming, experienced team driving past a small team of youngsters, or preferably youngsters with experienced leaders, will quickly teach the youngsters good practice.

A break for water also provides the opportunity to rest.
Pictured: Skiivolk Pepper.

WATER ROUTINES

As has been mentioned elsewhere, water has a critical role to play in the maintenance of healthy, active sled dogs. An important aspect of this is the use of water during training. It is good practice to always carry some water. This will not only allow you to provide a drink by means of a planned water stop during activity, but, should you have an unexpected stop which results in you being unable to complete your training run, you will be able to look after a potentially stressed team while help arrives with the truck.

The use of water has two major functions during training. It prevents the risk of unnecessary dehydration or overheating, and in addition it ensures that, following the two- or three-minute water break, the quality of the remainder of the training run is maintained following not only the rest, but also the intake of water.

A bucket with a lid acts as the best

water carrier. You should visit each pair of dogs in turn, allowing the dog to dip its head in once for a long drink. Once they raise their heads, you move on. You should go up the line twice allowing two dips; this should provide the right intake without risking any excessive intake.

Folk should not concern themselves that watering, which you can do once or twice on a run, will raise the teams' expectation of water during competition. Our experience is that race day is so different in so many ways from a day's training, that never is there any hint that dogs expect a water stop during competition. That said, it is sensible practice to vary where you stop to water on the trail, since constantly stopping in the same place will inevitably heighten expectations.

AREAS OF RISK
Apart from souring your dogs, excessive or thoughtless training can result in stiffness and general discomfort, jarring through the skeletal structure, stress fractures, stone bruising of the pads, grazes and abrasions, excessive nail wear, sore pasterns, heat stress and dehydration etc.

All these conditions can be avoided through good planning and preparation in advance and thinking 'dog' all the time!

After any hard exercise should come a special reward. A biscuit in a hot dog's mouth could not be less appropriate –

would you finish a five- to ten-mile run with a biscuit?

Following work, once they have been watered and rewarded, allow your dogs to cool down. If you have a large fenced facility allow them to loosen-off by encouraging them to run around.

After your main winter season activity, run your dogs down gradually, in the same way you built them up. You should gradually reduce both the number of outings back to say 8-10 a month, and the period of running time. Nothing could be worse than to stop a dog from all activity when he is at peak fitness, both physically and psychologically.

Dogs, young and old, will sometimes have line tangles while running. This is inevitable. Useful time can be spent encouraging the Siberian to get out of the tangle unaided, where possible. Gentle braking of the rig or sled will aid the dog concerned, but, given encouragement, dogs will quickly discover escape techniques.

Despite all your efforts to encourage your dogs to respond to the call of nature prior to work, they will inevitably want to go during running. Again, encouragement by the driver, and a little use of the brake without stopping will teach them that if, in future, they need to go, they can do so on the run, without fear of injury.

A comment regarding eager helpers, friends who want to be part of your routine but only on an infrequent basis.

Two points. Make sure the help received is beneficial to you and the dogs and does not result in you being thrown out of your routine and missing something. Secondly, make sure the dogs are comfortable with your helpers themselves, and are not just being thrown together with a non-doggy person!

TRAINING VENUES

An important factor in the training and conditioning of your team is your training area. It will also have a significant impact on the enjoyment your dogs have when working.

Variety is the spice of life they say, and this should be very much your goal when training dogs. While finding an area is sometimes tough, the ideal is to identify as many different trails and different hook-up points as possible. Different training areas, which present

both hill training combined with training on the flat, are also desirable.

Surface variation is also a factor. Fit feet are achieved not just by running on snow or grass or sand, but by running on a range of surfaces apart, of course, from concrete or asphalt. The number of teams we know who can run on softer, 'giving' trails but cannot perform on harder, faster, dirt trails, and vice versa, is always surprising. For those who do not have the benefit of good-quality year-round snow, and I guess that is the majority, your Siberians must develop feet that are tough enough to cope with a range of surfaces.

Teams that train constantly on flat trails lack the confidence to perform on hills; teams that only train on hills will lack the aptitude to work at a steady pace on flatter terrain.

Many drivers will limit themselves to

Training in a variety of locations provides the team with good experience for future races. Photo: Stu Forster.

Successful racing relies on the handler's versatility.

working in daylight, but an all-too-familiar trail will look completely different in the dark, with rig lights casting shadows, and the dogs chasing imaginary images on the trail ahead.

A trail that offers winding tracks and plenty of turns is far more appealing than long grinding straights which can drive a dog to total boredom.

Variety will benefit your team; hills and flats, soft and hard, day and night, snow and dirt, wet and dry – these will all provide the appropriate experience for your team, and will require of you even greater commitment if you are to provide this experience.

RACING

Ultimately, success on the race trail will depend on your ability to juggle the ingredients of successful sled dog racing – the breeding programme, the training and conditioning, nutrition, your equipment and your race strategy. Where competition is fierce, all these must come together if you are to achieve success.

One of the great aspects of this sport is that it is like a game of chess. You are faced with a new experience on each occasion you compete, and you must be flexible, and be prepared to analyse past performance in detail if you are to be able to make improvements and move forward.

Never run a race trail unless you have familiarised yourself with it beforehand. Arrive a day early and walk or drive the trail. In doing so you will also reduce the effect stress has on your dogs when travelling on the day of the race.

Prepare meticulously for the race. Check every detail of your race equipment. So often we have seen the best team of dogs fail not because of a dog issue, but because of equipment failure.

Complete your hard training two weeks before racing, and keep your team 'peaked' in preparation. Rest your team a full two days after a hard race, and then pick up with a fun run. Analyse the whole team's performance and learn.

5 THE BREED STANDARDS

The American Kennel Club published the first Standard for the Siberian Husky in 1930. Since then, many definitions have been altered, and this has affected how the breed has developed over the years. The European Breed Standards are derived from the American and Canadian Standards, and vary but little from the current AKC/CKC Standards. The Fédération Cynologique Internationale (FCI) Standard is the same as the AKC Standard.

THE ORIGINAL STANDARD

1930 AMERICAN KENNEL CLUB SIBERIAN HUSKY STANDARD

GENERAL APPEARANCE
For hundreds of years the Siberian Husky has been used as a sled dog in North Eastern Asia. He should be exceptionally active, quick and light on his feet, able to run in harness

Active, strong and light on his feet: the AKC Breed Standard has been emphasising the breed's working qualities since 1930.

with a load at a speed of twenty miles an hour for short distances. He should be strong, courageous and tireless on the trail. He should have a

PARTS OF THE DOG

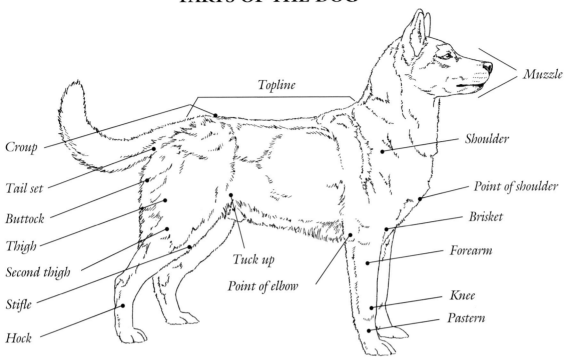

Topline

Muzzle

Croup

Tail set

Buttock

Thigh

Second thigh

Stifle

Hock

Tuck up

Point of elbow

Shoulder

Point of shoulder

Brisket

Forearm

Knee

Pastern

SKELETAL STRUCTURE

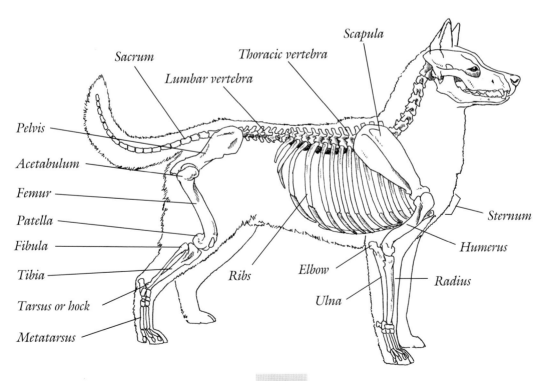

Scapula

Thoracic vertebra

Sacrum

Lumbar vertebra

Pelvis

Acetabulum

Femur

Patella

Fibula

Tibia

Tarsus or hock

Metatarsus

Ribs

Elbow

Ulna

Sternum

Humerus

Radius

71

deep strong chest, heavy bone, strong legs and feet, straight powerful back and well-muscled hindquarters. A grown dog should stand about 23 inches at the shoulders and weigh about 60 lbs. A bitch should be smaller and weigh about 10-12 lbs less.

HEAD
The size of the head should be in proportion to the body but not clumsy or too large. It should be of medium width between the ears. The ears should be erect, set high on the head, medium in size, pointed at the tops and well covered with hair on the inside. The head should be of medium length and slightly wedge-shaped. The jaws and teeth are very strong and should be neither overshot nor undershot. The eyes may be either blue or brown with a keen, friendly and intelligent expression. Eye rims dark. The nose may be either light brown or black. The muzzle should be strong, the lips dark and firmly fitting together.

CHEST AND RIBS
Chest should be deep and strong, but not too broad. The ribs should be well arched and deep.

BACK, QUARTERS AND STIFLES
The loins should be slightly arched and especially well muscled. The stifles should be well let down and especially well muscled. The back

should be straight, not too long, and strongly developed.

LEGS
Straight, of good length, well muscled and good bone.

FEET
Strong, not too compact, with exceptionally tough pads protected with hair.

TAIL
Long, and usually carried over back but sometimes dropped down, especially when tired. Should be well protected with fur and hair, but bushy tails not desirable.

SIZE AND WEIGHT
Dogs 22-23.5 inches at shoulder, 54-64 pounds; bitches 21-22.5 inches, 44-54 pounds.

COLOR
All colors permissible from white to black, including many variations of grays and mixed wolf colorings.

COAT
Should be thick with a very soft and warm underfur next to the skin. The guard hairs should not be too long, and should be straight, not too coarse, and fairly close to the body so that the graceful lines of the dog are not obscured. A bushy or shaggy coat is not desirable.

POINT SCALE

Size and general appearance	25pts
Head and Neck	10pts
Coat and Color	10pts
Chest and ribs	10pts
Quarters and Stifles	15pts
Back	10pts
Legs	10pts
Feet	5pts
Tail	5pts

THE CURRENT STANDARDS

THE AMERICAN KENNEL CLUB STANDARD 1990

(Reproduced by kind permission of the American Kennel Club)

GENERAL APPEARANCE

The Siberian Husky is a medium-sized working dog, quick and light on his feet and graceful in action. His moderately compact and well furred body, erect ears and brush tail suggest his Northern heritage. His characteristic gait is smooth and seemingly effortless. He performs his original function in harness most capably, carrying a light load at moderate speed over great distances. His body proportions and form reflect this basic balance of power, speed and endurance. The males of the Siberian Husky breed are masculine but never coarse, the bitches are feminine but without weakness of structure. In proper condition, with muscle firm and well developed, the Siberian Husky does not carry excess weight.

SIZE, PROPORTION, SUBSTANCE

Height: Dogs 21 to 23.5 inches at the withers. Bitches 20 to 22 inches at the withers.
Weight: Dogs 45 to 60 pounds. Bitches 35 to 50 pounds. Weight is in proportion to height.

The measurements mentioned above represent the extreme height and weight limits with no preference given to either extreme. Any appearance of excessive bone or weight should be penalized. In profile, the length of the body from the point of the shoulders to the rear point of the croup is slightly longer than the height of the body from the ground to the top of the withers. Disqualification: Dogs over 23.5 inches and bitches over 22 inches.

HEAD

Expression is keen, but friendly; interested and even mischievous. Eyes almond shaped, moderately spaced and set a trifle obliquely. Eyes may be brown or blue in color; one of each or parti-colored are acceptable. Faults: Eyes set too obliquely; set too close together.

Ears of medium size, triangular in shape, close fitting and set high on the head. They are thick, well furred,

The head should be in proportion to the body.

slightly arched at the back, and strongly erect, with slightly rounded tips pointing straight up.
Faults: Ears too large in proportion to the head; too wide set; not strongly erect.

Skull of medium size and in proportion to the body; slightly rounded on top and tapering from the widest point to the eyes.
Faults: Head clumsy or heavy; head too finely chiseled.

Stop: The stop is well defined and the bridge of the nose is straight from the stop to the tip.
Fault: Insufficient stop.

Muzzle of medium length; that is, the distance from the tip of the nose to the stop is equal to the distance from the stop to the occiput. The muzzle is of medium width, tapering

gradually to the nose, with the tip neither pointed nor square.
Faults: Muzzle either too snipy or too coarse; muzzle too short or too long.

Nose black in gray, tan or black dogs; liver in copper dogs; may be flesh colored in pure white dogs. The pink-streaked "snow nose" is acceptable.

Lips are well pigmented and close fitting.

Teeth closing in a scissors bite.
Fault: Any bite other than scissors.

NECK, TOPLINE, BODY
Neck medium in length, arched and carried proudly erect when dog is standing. When moving at a trot, the neck is extended so that the head is carried slightly forward.
Faults: Neck too short and thick; neck too long.

Chest deep and strong, but not too broad, with the deepest point being just behind and level with the elbows. The ribs are well sprung from the spine but flattened on the sides to allow for freedom of action.
Faults: Chest too broad; "barrel ribs"; ribs too flat or weak.

Back: The back is straight and strong, with a level topline from withers to croup. It is of medium length, neither cobby nor slack from excessive length. The loin is taut and lean, narrower than the rib cage, and

with a slight tuck-up. The croup slopes away from the spine at an angle, but never so steeply as to restrict the rearward thrust of the hind legs.
Faults: Weak or slack back; roached back; sloping topline.

TAIL

The well-furred tail of fox-brush shape is set on just below the level of the topline and is usually carried over the back in a graceful sickle curve up. The tail does not curl to either side of the body, nor does it snap flat against the back. A trailing tail is normal for

The tail is carried over the back in a graceful curve.

the dog when in repose. Hair on the tail is of medium length and approximately the same length on the top, sides and bottom giving the appearance of a round brush.
Faults: A snapped or tightly curled tail, highly plumed tail, tail set too low or too high.

FOREQUARTERS

Shoulders: The shoulder blade is well laid back. The upper arm angles slightly backward from point of shoulder to elbow, and is never perpendicular to the ground. The muscles and ligaments holding the shoulder to the rib cage are firm and well developed.
Faults: Straight shoulders; loose shoulders.

Forelegs: When standing and viewed from the front, the legs are moderately spaced, parallel and straight, with the elbows close to the body and turned neither in nor out. Viewed from the side, pasterns are slightly slanted, with the pastern joint strong, but flexible. Bone is substantial but never heavy. Length of the leg from elbow to ground is slightly more than the distance from the elbow to the top of the withers. Dewclaws on forelegs may be removed.
Faults: Weak pasterns, too heavy bone, too narrow or too wide in the front; out at the elbows.

Feet oval in shape but not long. The

paws are medium in size, compact and well furred between the toes and pads. The pads are tough and thickly cushioned. The paws neither turn in nor out when the dog is in natural stance.

Faults: Soft or splayed toes, paws too large and clumsy, paws too small and delicate; toeing in or out.

HINDQUARTERS

When standing and viewed from the rear, the hind legs are moderately spaced and parallel. The upper thighs are well muscled and powerful, the stifles well bent, the hock joint well defined and set low to the ground. Dewclaws, if any, are to be removed.

Faults: Straight stifles, cow-hocks, too narrow or too wide in the rear.

COAT

The coat of the Siberian Husky is double and medium in length, giving a well-furred appearance but is never so long as to obscure the clean-cut outline of the dog. The undercoat is soft and dense and of sufficient length to support the outer coat. The guard hairs of the outer coat are straight and somewhat smooth lying, never harsh nor standing straight off from the body. It should be noted that the absence of the undercoat during the shedding season is normal. Trimming of whiskers and fur between the toes and around the feet to present a neater appearance is permissible. Trimming

the fur on any other part of the dog is not to be condoned and should be severely penalized.

Faults: Long, rough or shaggy coat; texture too harsh or too silky; trimming of the coat, except as permitted above.

COLOR

All colors from black to pure white are allowed. A variety of markings on the head is common, including many striking patterns not found in other breeds.

GAIT

The Siberian Husky's characteristic gait is smooth and seemingly effortless. He is quick and light on his feet, and when in the show ring should be gaited on a loose lead at a moderately fast trot, exhibiting good reach in the forequarters and good drive in the hindquarters.

When viewed from the front to rear while moving at a walk the Siberian Husky does not single-track, but as the speed increases the legs gradually angle inward until the pads are falling on a line directly under the longitudinal center of the body. As the pad marks converge, the forelegs and hind legs are carried straightforward, with neither elbows nor stifles turned in or out. Each hind leg moves in the path of the foreleg on the same side. While the dog is gaiting the topline remains firm and level.

GAIT

Gait should be free, easy, and energy-efficient.

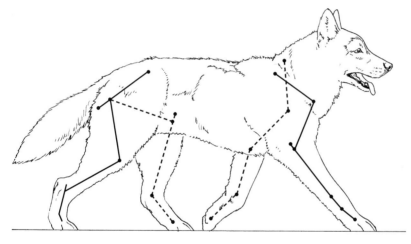

Bone angulation in a supported trot.

Faults: Short, prancing or choppy gait, lumbering or rolling gait; crossing or crabbing.

TEMPERAMENT

The characteristic temperament of the Siberian Husky is friendly and gentle, but also alert and outgoing. He does not display the possessive qualities of the guard dog, nor is he overly suspicious of strangers or aggressive with other dogs. Some measure of reserve and dignity may be expected in the mature dog.

His intelligence, tractability, and eager disposition make him an agreeable companion and willing worker.

SUMMARY

The most important breed characteristics of the Siberian Husky are medium size, moderate bone, well-balanced proportions, ease and freedom of movement, proper coat, pleasing head and ears, correct tail, and good disposition. Any appearance of excessive bone or weight, constricted or clumsy gait, or long, rough coat should be penalized. The Siberian Husky never appears so heavy or coarse as to suggest a freighting animal; nor is he so light and fragile as to suggest a sprint-racing animal. In both sexes the Siberian Husky gives the appearance of being capable of great endurance. In addition to the faults already noted, the obvious structural faults common to all breeds are as undesirable in the Siberian Husky as in any other breed, even though they are not specifically mentioned herein.

DISQUALIFICATION Dogs over 23.5 inches and bitches over 22 inches.

CANADIAN KENNEL CLUB STANDARD
(Reproduced by kind permission of the Canadian Kennel Club)

GENERAL APPEARANCE AND CONDUCT
The Siberian Husky is an alert, gracefully built, medium-sized dog, quick and light on his feet and free and graceful in action. He has a strong moderately compact body, a deep, strong chest, well-muscled shoulders and hindquarters and straight strong legs with medium bone. His coat is dense and very soft and his brush tail is carried curled over his back when at attention and trailing when in repose. His head presents a finely chiseled and often fox-like appearance and his eyes have a keen and friendly expression.

His characteristic gait is free, tireless and almost effortless when

Bitches (right) are smaller and more feminine-looking than dogs (left).

free or on a loose leash, but showing great strength when pulling, the trot is brisk and smooth and quite fast.

Bitches are smaller than dogs, averaging up to 2 inches shorter and 10 pounds less in weight. Siberians range in build from moderately compact (but never "cobby") to moderately rangy, in all builds the bone must be medium, the back powerful (never slack from excessive length), and the shoulder height never exceeding 23.5 inches. (Any ranginess is merely a matter of proportion, not of actual height).

HEAD

Skull: Of medium size in proportion to the body. Width between ears medium to narrow gradually tapering to eyes and moderately rounded. Muzzle of medium length. Both skull and muzzle are finely chiseled. Lips dark and close fitting, jaws and teeth strong, meeting with a scissors bite.

Ears: Of medium size, erect, close fitting, set high on head and well covered with hair on the inside. There is an arch at the back of the ears. Ears are slightly taller than width at base, and moderately rounded at tips. When dog is at attention ears are usually carried practically parallel on top of head, with inner edges quite close together at base.
Faults: Low-set ears; ears too large; "flat" ears; lop ears.

Eye colours vary – sometimes on the same dog!

Eyes: Either brown or blue ("watch" or "china") in color, one blue and one brown eye permissible but not preferable. Set only ever so slightly obliquely in skull. Eyes have a keen, friendly and fox-like expression; this expression is distinctly "interested", sometimes even mischievous.

Nose: Black for preference, brown allowed in occasional specimens of reddish coloring, flesh-colored nose and eye rims allowed in white dogs. Some dogs, especially black and white ones, have what is often termed a "snow nose" or "smudge nose", i.e. a nose normally solid black but acquiring a pink streak in winter. This is permissible but not preferable.

COAT

The Siberian Husky has a thick, soft double coat consisting of a soft, dense, downy undercoat of fur next to the skin and an outer coat of soft smooth texture giving a smooth, full-furred appearance and a clean-cut outline (in contrast to the harsh coarse coat of the Alaskan Malamute or the bear-like Eskimo coat). The coat is usually medium in length; a longer coat is allowed but the texture must remain the same in any length.
Faults: Any harshness (except while actually shedding); rough or shaggy appearance (like Samoyed, Malamute or Eskimo); absence of undercoat (except while shedding).

TAIL

A well-furred brush carried over back in a sickle curve while running or at attention and trailing when working or in repose. Tail should not "snap" flat to back. Hair on tail is usually of medium length, varying somewhat with the length of the dog's coat.

COLOR

All colors and white allowed, and all markings. The commonest colors are various shades of wolf and silver grays, tan (a light sable) and black with white points. A large variety of markings, especially head markings, are found in the Siberian, including many striking and unusual ones not found in any other breed. Frequently found are the cap-like mask and spectacle markings.

CHEST, RIBS, SHOULDERS

Chest should be deep and strong, but not too broad. Ribs should be well arched and deep. Shoulders well developed and powerful.
Faults: Chest too broad, (like Malamute); weak or flat chest; weak shoulders.

BACK, LOINS, QUARTERS

Back medium length, not too long nor cobby like the Elkhound, and strongly developed. Loins well muscled and slightly arched and should carry no excess weight or fat. Hindquarters powerful and showing good angulation.
Faults: Weak or slack back and weakness of hindquarters.

LEGS

Straight and well muscled with good bone (but never heavy bone like the Eskimo or Alaskan Malamute). Stifles well bent. Dewclaws occasionally appear on the hind legs. They are not a sign of impure breeding but as they interfere with the dog's work, they should be removed, preferably at birth.
Faults: Heavy bones; too light bone; lack of proper angulation in hind legs.

FEET

Oblong in shape and not so broad as

Standard fitting Siberian.

Non standard fitting: this dog displays many common faults – throatiness, overly deep chest, short legs, blunt head, straight topline, and heavy bone. It is "cobby like the Elkhound".

the Eskimo or Malamute, well furred between pads which are tough and thickly cushioned, compact, neither too large (like the Malamute) nor too small (like many Samoyeds). The Siberian's foot, like that of other true Arctic dogs, is a "snowshoe foot", i.e. it is somewhat webbed between the toes, like a Retriever's foot. Good feet are very important and, therefore, feet should always be examined in the ring.

Faults: Soft or splayed feet; feet too large or clumsy; feet too small or delicate.

HEIGHT
Dogs from 21 to 23.5 inches at the shoulder.
Bitches from 20 to 22 inches at the shoulder.

WEIGHT
Dogs from 45 to 60 pounds.
Bitches from 35 to 50 pounds.

Disqualification: Weight over 60 pounds in the male or over 50 pounds in the female. (Anything over these weights indicates cross-breeding). Height and weight are very important and the upper limit in each must be rigidly maintained.

THE BRITISH STANDARD 1986
(Reproduced by kind permission of the Kennel Club)

GENERAL APPEARANCE

Medium-sized working sled dog, quick and light on feet. Free and graceful in action, with well-furred body, erect ears and brush tail. Proportions reflect a basic balance of power, speed and endurance, never appearing so heavy or coarse as to suggest a freighting animal, nor so light and fragile as to suggest a sprint-racing animal. Males are masculine but never coarse, bitches feminine but without weakness of structure. Muscle firm and well developed, no excess weight.

Incorrect head – bulky, throaty, loose-lipped, with an exaggerated stop.

CHARACTERISTICS

Medium size, moderate bone, well-balanced proportions, ease and freedom of movement, and good disposition.

TEMPERAMENT

Friendly and gentle, alert and outgoing. Does not display traits of the guard dog, not suspicious with strangers or aggressive with dogs but some measure of reserve expected in mature dog. Intelligent, tractable and eager disposition. An agreeable companion and willing worker.

HEAD AND SKULL

Medium size in proportion to the body, presents a finely-chiselled fox-like appearance. Slightly rounded on top, tapering gradually from widest point to eyes. Muzzle medium length and width, neither snipy nor coarse, tapering gradually to rounded nose. Tip of nose to stop equidistant from stop to occiput. Stop clearly defined but not excessive. Nose black in grey, tan or black dogs; liver in copper dogs; and may be flesh-coloured in pure white. In winter, pink-streaked ("snow nose") is acceptable.

The almond-shaped eyes should have a keen expression.

Correct ear set.

EYES
Almond-shaped, moderately spaced and set obliquely. Any shade of blue or brown, one of each colour, or parti-colours equally acceptable. Expression keen, but friendly, interested, even mischievous.

EARS
Medium size, relatively close together, triangular in shape, the height slightly greater than width at base. Set high on head, strongly erect, the inner edges being quite close together at the base, when the dog is at attention carried practically parallel. Slightly arched at the back. Thick, well furred outside and inside, tips slightly rounded.

MOUTH
Lips well pigmented, close fitting. Jaws strong, with a perfect regular and complete scissor bite, i.e. upper teeth closely overlapping lower teeth and set square to the jaws.

NECK
Medium length and thickness, arched and carried proudly erect when standing. When moving at a trot, extended so that the head is carried slightly forward.

FOREQUARTERS
Shoulder blade well laid back, upper arm angles slightly backward from point of shoulder to elbow, never perpendicular to the ground. Muscle holding shoulder to rib cage firm and well developed. Straight or loose shoulders highly undesirable. Viewed from the front, forelegs moderately spaced, parallel and straight with elbows close to the body, turning neither in nor out. Viewed from the side, pasterns slightly sloping, wrist strong but flexible. Length from elbow to ground slightly more than distance from elbows to top of withers. Bone proportionate, never heavy. Dewclaws may be removed.

BODY
Straight and strong, with level topline from withers to croup. Medium length, not cobby, nor slack from excessive length. In profile, body from point of shoulder to rear point of croup slightly longer than height from ground to top of withers. Chest deep and strong but

not too broad, deepest point being just behind and level with elbows. Ribs well sprung from spine but flattened on sides to allow for freedom of action. Loins slightly arched, well muscled, taut and lean, narrower than rib cage with a slight tuck-up. Croup slopes away from spine at an angle, but never so steeply as to restrict the rearward thrust of hind legs.

HINDQUARTERS
Viewed from rear, hind legs moderately spaced and parallel. Upper thighs well muscled and powerful, stifles well bent, hock joint well defined and set low to ground. Dewclaws, if any, should be removed.

FEET
Oval, not long, turning neither in nor out in natural stance. Medium size, compact, well furred and slightly webbed between toes. Pads tough and thickly cushioned. Trimming of fur between toes and around feet permissible.

TAIL
Well furred, of round, fox brush shape set on just below level of topline and usually carried over back in graceful sickle curve when dog at attention. When carried up, tail should not curl too tightly, nor should it curl to either side of body, or snap flat against back. Hair on tail

of medium length and approximately same length all round. A trailing tail is normal for the dog when working or in repose.

GAIT/MOVEMENT
Smooth and seemingly effortless. Quick and light on feet, gaited on a loose lead at a moderately fast trot, exhibiting good reach in forequarters and good drive in hindquarters. When walking, legs move in parallel, but as speed increases, gradually angling inward to single track. As pad marks converge, forelegs and hindlegs carried straight with neither elbows nor stifles turning in nor out, each hindleg moving in path of foreleg on same side. Topline of back remaining firm and level during gaiting.

COAT
Double, and medium in length, giving a well-furred appearance, never so long as to obscure clean-cut outline of dog. Undercoat soft and dense; of sufficient length to support outer coat. Guard hairs of outer coat straight and somewhat smooth-lying, never harsh, rough or shaggy, too silky nor standing straight off from body. Absence of undercoat during shedding normal. No trimming of fur on any part of dog, except feet.

COLOUR
All colours and markings, including

84

white, allowed. Variety of markings on head is common, including many striking patterns not found in other breeds.

SIZE
Height: dogs: 53-60 cm (21-23.5 ins) at withers; bitches: 51-56 cm (20-22 ins) at withers.
Weight: dogs: 20-27 kgs (45-60 lbs); bitches: 16-23 kgs (35-50 lbs). Weight should be in proportion to height.
These measurements represent the extremes in height and weight, with no preference given to either extreme. A dog should not exceed 60 cms (23.5 ins) or a bitch exceed 56 cms (22 ins).

FAULTS: Any departure from the foregoing points should be considered a fault and the seriousness with which the fault should be regarded should be in exact proportion to its degree.

NOTE: Male animals should have two apparently normal testicles fully descended into the scrotum.

INTERPRETING THE STANDARDS
Since the first Standard was adopted by the AKC in 1930, many definitions have changed, particularly with regard to head shape, eye colour, weight, tail-carriage and coat colours. These changes have been made in an attempt to clarify what can be difficult wording. It is impossible to describe an animal well enough, via the printed word, so that all readers and judges interpret that description in the same way.

GENERAL APPEARANCE
This section gives an overview of the Siberian Husky, referring to his medium size, balanced proportions, moderate bone, ease and freedom of movement and friendly disposition. Siberians can vary in build from moderately compact to moderately rangey. 'Rangey', often defined as long and slender, is an expression sometimes used when describing a Husky in outline. This description for the Siberian should indicate length approximately 10 per cent greater than height, with a tendency towards squareness at one extreme or excessive back length at the other – both being undesirable.

This balance is fundamental in providing power, speed and endurance. There is an impression of great strength and fitness, a strong chest, well-muscled quarters, strong legs but of medium bone. The Siberian should be alert, quick and light on his feet, never heavy-set, cloddy, slow in his movement or indifferent to his surroundings.

TEMPERAMENT
The Standards are very clear on this issue. The excitement and enthusiasm, so evident at hook-up, is often offset by Siberians' laid-back but friendly and

Correct: Moderate stop.   *Incorrect: Excessive stop.*   *Incorrect: Insufficient stop.*

outgoing attitude in the show ring. The typical Siberian will be able to cope with both situations; nervousness may be accommodated while running in big teams, but any hint of an aggressive tendency is absolutely undesirable.

HEAD AND SKULL

The head should be medium in size and in proportion to the body. Any coarseness generally evident in the head often reflects heavy bone (round) as opposed to medium bone (oval and strong). The description "finely chiselled and fox-like appearance" aptly describes the Siberian head: this description sadly was taken out of the AKC Standard in 1972. The muzzle should be medium in length; too short and cold air will not be properly warmed before reaching the sinuses and lungs. There should be an equal distance between the occiput and the stop, and the stop and the tip of the nose.

EARS

The descriptions in the Standards seem to allow for great variation in the breed. A Siberian's ears are very mobile in reacting to stimuli but, when alert, they become close at the base if high set, with almost parallel inside lines. Ears generally vary in size and are deemed correct if they are in balance with the head, but they can greatly detract from the typical expression if incorrect.

EYES

Almond-shaped, moderately spaced and set a trifle obliquely. Level-set eyes do not provide a keen expression and tend to give an impression of disinterest, quite unlike the often mischievous expression. It is important for the eyes to be the correct shape and set obliquely as this is said to help protect them from driving winds and snow. All eye colours are acceptable. This variety is a unique feature of the breed.

THE EARS

Correct: ear size and set.   *Incorrect: ears too small.*   *Incorrect: ears too large.*

MOUTH

The Standards call for a correct scissor bite. The position, shape and size of the jaws can affect the looseness of the lips and flews. A loose lip line will spoil the whole appearance of the face, losing the refined appearance.

NECK

A Siberian with a good reach of neck looks beautiful in side profile when standing. Interestingly, the head of a good dog should lower and be level with the back when running in harness. If not, it is generally shorter in reach. The Siberian also lowers the head when trotting on a loose lead in the show ring, but, if it is 'strung up' while gaiting, it will have a choppy or hackney movement which spoils its free stride.

FOREQUARTERS

Well-laid shoulders are a key component of the Siberian's conformation. The scapula should be at an angle of 30-40 degrees, the ideal being 35 degrees. The scapula and humerus should be of equal length. Spacing between the shoulders at the withers should be at least two inches. For good shoulder placement the dog must have broad, long shoulder blades, attached by strong muscles to the rib cage. The ribs are well laid back. All too often we see short, straight upper arms with too little reach in front movement. Leg length should be 1.2 to 1.25 times the chest depth, so it is worth emphasising that the distance from elbow to ground should be greater than the distance from elbow to top of withers. It is important to check this with 'hands on', as coat is deceptive. There has never been a dog with a chest which extends below the level of the elbow that can run efficiently. The bone should be oval and not round, as is seen in the majority of heavier dogs.

LEGS, FEET AND FORELEGS

The legs are straight and strong (oval bone, not round) moderately spaced (a hand's width at the chest) and parallel, with elbows close to the body.

When standing, the front feet should be angled outward at about 10 degrees (toeing out). This is important because, when the dog moves and his feet swing inwards under the centre of gravity, the action will be off his centre toes, with the small toes being used only for balance on turns. Feet that are straight

Legs are straight and strong with feet angled outward at about 180 degrees.

ahead when standing cannot be rotated properly when swung inward – causing the action to come off one centre toe and one small toe – providing less efficient movement.

Viewed from the side, the pastern is long and angled backward (10 degrees to 15 degrees) giving flexibility and allowing a greater reach in stride. Short and straight pasterns cause a very tight, restricted action. The feet should be oval in shape, toes well arched, the paws well muscled, medium in size, compact and well furred between the toes and pads. The pads should be well cushioned and tough. Well-formed feet are important for their potential speed and endurance.

Poor feet can, at one extreme, be referred to as 'cat feet' which are small and round in shape, and at the other extreme may be referred to as 'hare feet' which are recognised as having overly long toes. The modified hare foot, which is the ideal between the two, is oval in shape, is well cushioned and is well knuckled up when fit.

Pad pigmentation varies: lemon and black are often associated with a tougher pad than a pink pad.

BODY AND BACK

The back of the dog is made up of thoracic and lumbar vertebrae. It slopes slightly down from the tip of the withers to the mid-back and then rises again over the loin and then slopes down a little towards the croup. It is critical that the back is flexible enough

The back must be strong and flexible.

to co-ordinate front and rear assemblies when on the move and yet strong enough to support the internal organs.

Many people misunderstand the necessity of flexibility and quite literally take the Standards' interpretation of level top line as being straight from withers to croup. To achieve this, everything is shortened, generally achieving a 'cobby' type with a short loin. The front and rear angulation is also affected, causing a short, choppy gait. The chest depth is the strength, with the deepest point being just behind the elbow. The oval rib cage extends to more than half the overall body length with flattened sides allowing for maximum heart and lung room without impeding the free, straight movement of the front legs, i.e. in no way round or barrel-ribbed.

The length of the back (breastbone to end of croup) should be around 10 to 15 per cent longer than height (ground to withers). This presents a rectangular shape of daylight under the dog.

The arched loin should be taut and lean, narrower than the rib cage, with a definite tuck-up. The loin has to be strong, yet supple for galloping. It is clear that if the loin was level, it would be inadequate for its function and it is important, therefore, that the loin should be slightly arched.

The croup slopes away from the spine at an angle of around 35 degrees. The correct slope of the pelvis is essential, as the power from the foot, travelling through the limb to the femur, has to be transmitted through the pelvis to the spine in as direct a line as possible. For optimum efficiency the slope of the pelvis should be between 30 and 35 degrees.

The Siberian should not carry any excess weight and should be shown in working condition, i.e. lean and hard.

HINDQUARTERS

The hindquarters should be in balance with the forequarters and, when viewed from the rear, the width equals the width of the shoulders. Correctly angulated and well proportioned, the hindquarters will provide the strong driving power so essential to the Siberian sled dog.

The muscles, which bind the leg to the hip, should be strong and well conditioned. Often seen are dogs which have a short and straight stifle which will greatly affect their running ability and shorten stride length. Weakness in the rear structure is also commonly seen when a dog stands 'cow hocked' and moves closely, when viewed from the

CORRECT TAIL CARRIAGE

TAIL FAULTS

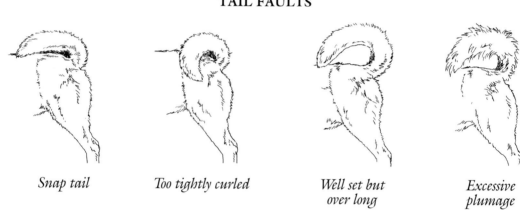

Snap tail   *Too tightly curled*   *Well set but over long*   *Excessive plumage*

rear, when trotting. Many think this is single tracking! Often a well-muscled Siberian, who is worked regularly, starts off moving wide for several paces when viewed from behind. This is a habit resulting from leaning into the harness at sled or rig release during work and should not be penalised in the show ring.

TAIL
The well-furred tail is set on the croup just below the level of the top line. The Standards state, "usually carried over the back in a graceful sickle curve when at attention" but the Siberian may carry it up or down and this should be

remembered when assessing or judging. When carried up, the tail should not curl to one particular side of the body, nor should it 'snap' against the back. A tight or 'snapped' tail usually indicates an incorrect slope to the pelvis. A trailing tail is normal for the dog when working or in repose. The length of the bone of the tail should reach the tip of the hock when the dog is standing.

TAIL SET VERSUS TAIL CARRIAGE
Not all tail faults affect the rear structure and this needs to be carefully assessed. It is often the visual appearance that can give the impression of a structural

90

The Siberian is an impressive mover; the gait should be smooth and effortless.

problem somewhere. Looking at the balance of the dog allows an assessment of why the tail is incorrect. If a tail is overly long and touches the back, the dog's structure may still be correct, but if a tail is carried too tightly because the dog has a short loin coupled with a short, flat croup, this would severely restrict rear movement and should be penalised.

THE GAIT

The Siberian Husky's characteristic gait is smooth and seemingly effortless. The most efficient gaits for the Siberian are the trot and the lope. The Siberian in the show ring should be gaited on a loose lead at a moderately fast trot. This movement should cover the ground easily with no wasted energy.

There is a tendency to present the Siberian as a flashy trotter in the show ring, and some are gaited incorrectly by stringing the dog up, therefore inducing an unnatural gait. The dog naturally should be quick and light on his feet, with the head extended and a firm and level top line, and no lateral movement. It is important to note that, as speed increases, the legs should angle inward until the pads are falling on a line directly under the longitudinal centre of the body. As the pad marks converge, the forelegs and hind legs are carried straight forward with neither elbows nor stifles turned in or out. The back feet should fill the 'holes' left by the front feet as the Siberian is gaited.

COAT

The coat is an important aspect of breed type. The Siberian has a double coat, with a soft, downy very dense undercoat, which is waterproof. The outer coat, or guard hair, is strong and soft, emerging from the follicles at 30 degrees to the skin to produce a full-furred, well-protected appearance. The Standards call for a double and medium length, which is vague and allows for some variation. A range of coat lengths is quite acceptable in the Siberian. A shorter, plush, dense type of coat is seen, which only becomes unacceptable if it is too short or unsupported by undercoat. The other extreme is a longer, stand-off coat. This can be deceptive and may make the dog appear heavier and bulkier than he in fact is, which is unacceptable if it obscures the clean-cut outline of the dog.

Texture of the coat is also important: a good Siberian coat is soft, dense and plush and is naturally clean. Should sand or grit get in the coat, after a few hours it will simply drop out. Remaining clean, of course, is essential to preserve the coat's insulating properties. Harsh, wiry coats do not repel dirt in this way and are incorrect. Waviness and silkiness are also incorrect. Waviness is generally evident along the top of the back and dogs with silky, over-fine textured coats often have feathering behind the ears.

A short undercoat which does not support the guard hairs, often termed as an 'open coat', is one of the worst types because it affords no protection against the wind, snow and freezing rain. The Standards also make it clear that the absence of undercoat during shedding is perfectly normal, but uneven shedding can make it difficult for the judge to make an assessment. The Standards comment that there should be no trimming of fur on any part of the dog, except feet. It should be quite unnecessary to trim a dog at all. The Siberian in his correct natural state should not need even his feet trimmed if he is properly exercised. Any evidence of fur trimming other than around the feet should be severely penalised since it is an attempt to cover up a major fault.

COLOUR

Many judges find it difficult to assess dogs with unusual markings, and with a wide variety of coat and eye colours, but breeding for colour preferences can only lose some of the more important aspects of the breed, including working attitude.

Many of the original dogs brought into Alaska for working and racing were white or piebald (dogs with uneven patches of colour on the body, but usually a distinctive facial mask) and many are still seen in predominantly working bloodlines. It is unfortunate that fashion can markedly alter a breed. The traditional Irish markings, black and white with blue eyes, were a craze for a long time in the US. However, other colour types, such as solid masks without a splash of white, are equally acceptable, while agouti (a mixture of grey and red shades on coloured areas), red and fawn sable are all within the Breed Standards.

SIZE AND HEIGHT

Height: Dogs: 53 to 60 cm (21 to 23.5 ins) at withers. Bitches: 51 to 56 cm (20 to 22 ins) at withers.

It is interesting that the Standards accommodate quite a range in size. The smallest is 20 inches for bitches and the largest is 23.5 inches for dogs. It is worth mentioning that, when confronted with such a range, it can be deceiving and difficult. If you have a ring full of dogs at the top of the Standard, with possibly a few oversized, it can make you think that the smallest in the line is too small. But it may well be perfectly acceptable. The same applies the other way around. It is worth having a good idea of the acceptable size range before judging or assessing.

Weight is another extremely important point. It should be in proportion to height. If a dog is over 60 lbs and 23.5 tall, this could be due to carrying too much weight coupled with heavy bone, both outside the Standards.

COLOUR

The variety of colours and patterns is remarkable, each one producing a stunning-looking dog.

Grey/white.

Fawn sable.

Black/grey/brown/white.

Wolf grey/brown/white.

6 SIBERIAN HUSKIES IN THE SHOW RING

Showing your Siberian can be a very enjoyable experience but it can also be a very frustrating one, so remember the golden rule – do not take it too seriously! Many people find that, during their first year or so of showing, they attend anything and everything that is available, going from show to show and spending a fortune on entry fees and petrol. If they win, then showing is the best hobby around; but, if they lose then the whole thing becomes a big bore – or worse!

The best way to avoid such disappointments is to take the whole thing less seriously in the first place. Enjoy a day out with friends, chat about Siberians and relax with your dog – after all, it is meant to be fun. Go to just a few shows and try all levels of shows. By doing that you can decide what you enjoy most and select accordingly: hopefully neither you nor your dog will get frustrated.

The charismatic Siberian has a natural presence in the ring.

GETTING STARTED

Shows are advertised in dog magazines and newspapers and also in local papers, depending on their size. Once you have

Showing your Siberian can be a rewarding hobby.

located the show, you will need to contact the organiser for further details. These generally come in the form of a schedule which lists the breeds and classes on offer, gives definitions of classes and the details of times, prices, judges etc. It will give a date by which all entries must be made. Make sure you comply with this.

Entry forms, which are included with the schedule, are self-explanatory but you will need details of your dog's parents and his breeder, and you may also need the dog's registration number. When you return the form and payment, many people recommend sending a self-addressed postcard too, so that the organiser can confirm receipt of your entry. It could be very disappointing to turn up and find your entry failed to arrive!

Rules vary from country to country. In Britain, entries are accepted up until the specified closing date, while, in the USA, entries frequently close as soon as the venue reaches capacity, so a speedy response is required.

WHAT CLASS?
Generally speaking, and certainly when you are starting out, you should enter the lowest class for which your dog is eligible. Classes are defined according to previous show wins of the dog, and the age of the dog. So, if you have an eight-month-old puppy, he should be entered according to his age, and, if you have a dog that has already won a number of classes, you may only be able to enter him in the higher classes. All classes are clearly defined in the schedule but, if in doubt, ask a friend or contact the show organiser.

There is one major difference between the USA and Britain. In the USA, dogs which have become Champions move into their own class while, in Britain, dogs wishing to become Champions still have to compete against existing Champions in the Open and Veteran classes.

TYPES OF SHOWS
These vary from country to country, but they range from the shows held on village playing fields, at garden fetes and summer shows in aid of charity, right up to Crufts and Westminster. Where you decide to compete will depend on you and your dog. Some people prefer the relaxed atmosphere of a show where you

enter on the day and mix with all breeds and crossbreeds, while others are only satisfied with the competition for Challenge Certificates and Best in Show at Championship shows. For many, a mixture is the answer. As long as you and your dog enjoy yourselves, it really does not matter.

Crufts is the largest and arguably the most prestigious dog show in the world, with more than 21,000 dogs competing for the Best in Show title. Dogs have to qualify for Crufts by winning at Championship shows. The show is run by The Kennel Club. Most British exhibitors aspire to enter their dogs at Crufts and, with the new quarantine regulations, this is also possible for some overseas competitors.

Westminster is the most important show in the USA. It takes place over two days in New York's Westminster halls, and has been held annually since 1907. The show is limited to dogs that have earned their AKC Championship and attracts an entry of more than 2,500. A total of 25,000 spectators visit the show to view more than 150 breeds and, like Crufts, it gives breeders the opportunity to extol the virtues of their particular breed and explain the advantages of owning pure-bred dogs. A Siberian Husky has won Best In Show on just one occasion – in 1980 the title was awarded to Kathleen Kanzler's Ch. Innisfree's Sierra Cinnar.

SHOW-RING PREPARATION

Siberian Huskies are one of the easiest breeds to prepare in terms of grooming. Preparing, in terms of training, takes a little more time and effort. Having paid to enter the show, gone to the expense of travelling there, and invested so much time and trouble in attending, it would seem to go without saying that preparing your dog properly is of paramount importance. Yet, and it never ceases to amaze us, we still see poorly groomed and frankly dirty dogs in the ring. This is an insult to both the judge and your dog.

It is well worthwhile getting your puppy or youngster accustomed to being bathed long before he attends his first show. Struggling and shaking Siberians can soak you from a good distance away but dogs who have been used to being bathed from a young age are easy to handle and confident in the bath. The process of bathing is covered elsewhere in this book but, suffice to say, once bathed, your dog will look extra-special for the ring if you can use a 'blaster' and drier in order to give the coat a really thorough dry. Longer-coated dogs should be

Practising the show stance at home will ensure it is second nature to your dog.

Work on your dog's coat before you get to the show – and then give a quick brush through before entering the ring.

bathed a few days before a show in order to let the coat settle again but shorter-coated dogs can be done the day before and look really good. Give a good brushing once the coat is dry and then all you will have to do is give a quick brush over before you go into the ring.

Siberians in the UK are shown 'au naturel' with the whiskers still in place and the coat untrimmed except for, perhaps, a slight trimming around the feet to give them a smooth outline. Using a pair of curved-ended scissors is the safest for this purpose. Trim away long hair under the foot and then just trim neatly round the edge with the foot flat on the floor. Do not overdo it!

In the USA, it is usual to trim the whiskers and sometimes the underside of the tail and chest. If your dog needs his nails trimmed, then you should be giving him more exercise. Very few well-exercised Siberians need any form of nail

clipping and the practice of clipping the nails above the quick, which causes pain and bleeding, is totally abhorrent to most of us and certainly should not be done to a Siberian, because he needs his nails for grip and turn when running.

TRANSPORTATION

As with anything you do with your dog, preparation is the key to success. If your puppy becomes accustomed to travelling from his early days, even if it is just a trip round the block in the car once a week, travelling will not be a problem. Generally, Siberians are the easiest of travellers and enjoy going to new places and meeting new dogs and people.

Siberian enthusiasts who have a number of dogs often have vans specially kitted out with carrying crates. For the one-dog owner travelling to a show, the dog will travel happily either on the back seat of the car (preferably wearing a dog car harness so he cannot fall forward if you brake suddenly), or in the back of an estate car (station wagon). But you must ensure that there is sufficient shade. How often have you seen owners travelling happily in the front of the car totally oblivious to the fact that the dog is being subjected to direct sunlight in the very back? Sunshades on the windows and plenty of ventilation resolve the problem. Air conditioning is even better.

ARRIVING AT THE SHOW

Allow plenty of time for your journey and arrive early. This is so much more relaxing than leaving it all until the last minute, having to queue in traffic to get into the show ground and arriving hot and flustered at your bench, worried that you have missed your class.

On arriving at the show, take your dog out of the car and allow him to answer the call of nature before you proceed to the show itself – this way everyone is comfortable before proceeding. You should have your passes ready to show at the entrance gate. On this will generally be printed your bench number and you will be directed to the benching area. When you finally find your bench, which is often the most stressful bit of the day, you will need a benching chain to attach to your dog's collar. *Never* use a check chain to bench your dog, as he could easily strangle himself. Use a wide-buckle collar (one-inch is best for a Siberian) and a fairly short benching chain, one which is long enough to allow him to lie down but not so long that he can step off the bench. Some exhibitors like to place rugs and towels on the benches, but this is a matter of choice.

At some shows, ring cards (the number card which you need to identify your dog in the ring) are placed on the bench, so you need to retrieve this immediately. At other shows, the cards are handed out in the ring, and some are even sent in the post beforehand. You will need your card in order to enter your class.

HANDLING
Your dog should already be clean and

Accustom your Siberian to being handled by strangers, so he does not resent the judge's attentions.

groomed before you arrive at the show, so at this point all you need to do is run a quick brush over him to make sure he is tidy. This is particularly important if he is moulting. At this point I should also add that getting your dog ready and then arriving in the ring looking a mess yourself completely ruins the picture! Although the judge is assessing the dog, not you, you will show off your dog to his best advantage if you take the trouble to wear tidy clothes, brush your hair and make yourself look the part. Over-dressing, however, is not necessary.

Take your dog off the bench while the class prior to yours is still being judged. Put on his show collar and lead. Make sure you have put on your ring card clip, take your bait and head for the ring. Pause en route in an exercise area for your dog to perform if necessary.

Hopefully you will have already done some ringcraft training either at home or at a weekly club. Siberians should be shown naturally. That means they should be on a loose lead. They do not need to be 'strung up' on a tight lead, or stacked, which means being manually stood and held in position. If your dog is a good example of the breed and has been properly trained, he will free-stand happily, showing himself off to the very best advantage, waiting to be given the odd treat, and then will move round the ring as requested by the judge.

He should also be accustomed to having his mouth handled. This is useful when going to the vet, as well as being essential in the ring where the judge will want to take a look at his teeth and his bite.

IN THE RING
When you are in the ring waiting to be judged, allow your dog to relax. Nothing looks worse, or sickens a dog of showing more quickly, than continually asking him to maintain concentration when there is no need. Showing should be fun for everyone – not least the dog. Watch the judge and see what he is asking each exhibitor to do, whether it is to move the dog in a triangle or circle, straight up and down. By observing these instructions you will be prepared when it comes to your turn.

When you move your dog, gather up the loose end of the lead into the palm of your hand. Do not leave it dangling over the dog's head as this is distracting for the judge and spoils the overall picture you are presenting. Handling is an important part of the whole process of

Watch the other exhibitors and listen carefully to the judge so you know how he wants you to move your dog.

showing and you should not simply turn up at your first show without having done any groundwork.

If you have trained your puppy from an early age to stand for food and to accept having his mouth handled, then you are halfway there. Get your puppy used to wearing a show lead – his normal lead will look heavy in the ring. Check chains are also a bad idea unless you are an expert in their use, so go for a narrow nylon half-check or similar. A colour which 'tones in' with your dog's coat is best.

The class will line up down one side of the ring and each dog will be seen in turn. Generally, this involves bringing the dog out and standing him for the judge to 'go over'. Reassure him while this is done but do not get in the judge's way. You will then be asked to move your dog. If you have been watching other classes, you will know what to do.

Never impede the judge's view of your dog – keep the dog between you and the

The moment of truth: unlike racing, judging is very much a subjective experience.

judge and keep yourself out of the way. Keeping your dog alert when the judge is viewing him, but allowing him to relax the rest of the time, will maintain your dog's interest.

'Fancy' handling is unnecessary and has no place in the normal show ring – those who wish to practise it as an art form in its own right may do so in specific handling competitions. For the show ring, the handler should be unobtrusive and should concentrate on showing the dog off to his best advantage.

WINNING AND LOSING
Win or lose, we all take the best dog, our friend, home with us. So it really does not matter who wins, but people still get very worked up over it. In the end, you have to bear in mind that what the judge is doing is simply giving an opinion, and that you will get a different opinion from a different judge. This is why many Siberian owners are happier racing their

dogs because you cannot argue with a clock: you either win or you don't – there are no opinions involved. Whether you win or lose, do it graciously. No one likes a 'big-head' or a poor loser, so you need to learn to carry off either with equanimity. And if you lose, remember it is not your dog's fault – it makes no difference to him and he certainly will not understand if you are suddenly in a bad mood with him!

SIBERIAN MISCHIEF
Dog shows should be a fun day out and, if either you or your dog do not enjoy them, then why do it? Most Siberians love shows and it is amazing that the dog which pulls like crazy in harness or on the lead when out walking, suddenly walks beautifully on the end of the lead when in the show ring. The one thing to bear in mind, though, is that Siberians can be mischievous in the ring and play up, bouncing about on the end of the lead and laughing at you and everyone else. This is very frustrating for the owner. It seems that all your hard work and training goes out of the window. But do not get upset or you will make things worse. Keep calm, stand still and make your dog start again from the beginning. This is very tedious for a dog that wants to play around and is usually effective.

Staying awake all day at a show is exciting and tiring and most Siberians will come home and sleep deeply to make up for their lost day's rest!

JUDGING

A specialist working breed like the Siberian needs to be judged by breed specialists as well as all-rounder judges. All-rounders, by the very fact that they judge a number of breeds, tend to see Siberians as show dogs and do not always appreciate the importance of their conformation if they are to function as a sled dog. If they consider the breed's working heritage and functional needs, they tend to look for a heavier type of dog, imagining that a freighting type is required, rather than the lightweight working dog which the Siberian was intended to be. This is not to criticise the all-rounder but simply to point out the need for this type of judge to be balanced by breed specialists.

Good judges should start from the bottom and work up. Judging the fun classes at local exemption shows and moving on to smaller, then larger, open shows will give you some of the experience you need. It is also essential to attend breed judging seminars and look at many different types of dog, both standing and on the move, and also relate this to how they move when running in harness.

Stewarding for other judges will help greatly, as standing in the ring with the dogs, in as near to the position of the judge as possible, gives a much more accurate view of the dogs than sitting at

When judging the Siberian, it is important to view the breed as a working dog.

the ringside. Stewarding for other breeds is also an excellent way to gain experience. Formal judging courses are available. These can be studied over a period and include 'hands-on' training as well as a great deal of theory. Such courses are well worth doing, whether you want to judge a number of breeds or just Siberian Huskies.

THE SHOW BAG CHECK LIST

- Passes and schedule (includes map to find the show)
- Brush and comb
- Water and bowl
- Ring card clip
- Show lead
- Treats
- Towel
- Benching chain
- Food – dog and human

7 HEALTH CARE AND HEREDITARY CONDITIONS

INTERNAL PARASITES

Internal parasites vary from country to country, with roundworms and tapeworms of different varieties being the most common. Roundworms (Toxocara) have a complicated life cycle that makes them very successful in infecting puppies. The larvae invade the body tissues of both pups and adults. They remain dormant until about two-thirds of the way through the dam's pregnancy, when they migrate into the foetuses, in the uterus, and develop in the bowel. Puppies also ingest worm eggs along with their mother's milk and can pick them up from contaminated surroundings. Advice about medication should be sought from your vet before whelping, both for dosing the mother and for the treatment of very young puppies. Regular treatment of both puppies and mother is essential to break the cycle but even adult dogs should continue to be treated six-monthly or annually to deal with any subsequent infestations they may pick up.

Treatment for tapeworm, heartworm, lungworm etc. should also be carried out at regular intervals according to the country you live in – discuss what is necessary with your vet.

EXTERNAL PARASITES

Fleas and ticks are the bane of any dog- and cat-owning household, particularly if you live and exercise your dogs in sheep or deer country. Tests have shown that the vast majority of fleas found on dogs are in fact cat fleas, so if you do have cats too, even if they live separately from the dogs, you will need to ensure that they remain flea-free too.

Flea treatments range from sprays, to collars, to powders and shampoos and from herbal to chemical, internal to external. It is also essential to treat living areas, vacuuming carpets regularly and washing bedding at the same time, otherwise, even though your pets are clear, they will immediately be

ROUNDWORM LIFE CYCLE

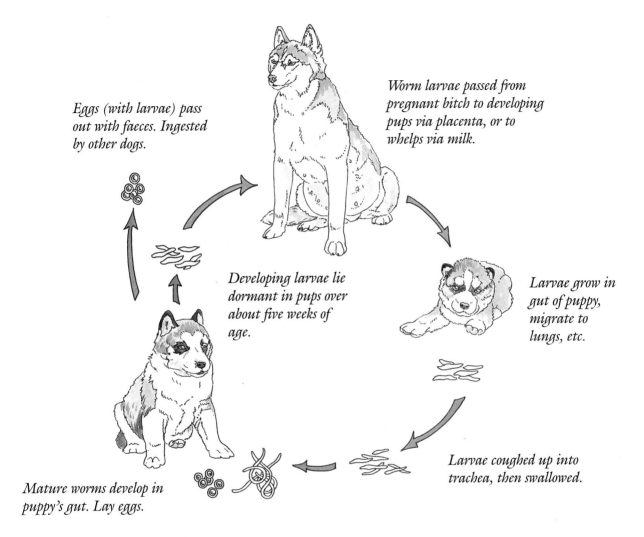

Eggs (with larvae) pass out with faeces. Ingested by other dogs.

Worm larvae passed from pregnant bitch to developing pups via placenta, or to whelps via milk.

Developing larvae lie dormant in pups over about five weeks of age.

Larvae grow in gut of puppy, migrate to lungs, etc.

Larvae coughed up into trachea, then swallowed.

Mature worms develop in puppy's gut. Lay eggs.

reinfested. What you use is up to you and to your vet, but you should certainly act quickly if you find evidence of fleas, or things can rapidly get worse.

Ticks are only a problem in certain areas but once again they should be dealt with speedily. Both fleas and ticks can be carriers of diseases which they can pass on to dogs – the diseases vary according to the host species and according to the part of the world in which they are found. Some of these diseases can be fatal but there are vaccines available in some countries where there is a need to protect from particular illnesses. You should discuss this with your vet.

Numerous methods of removing ticks are suggested including applying oil to the body, spraying with flea and tick

TAPEWORM LIFE CYCLE

Dog eats flea (with immature worms inside) whilst grooming.

Flea larva develops and matures with immature worms inside.

Worm matures in dog's gut.

Segments break off, and are passed out with faeces.

Flea larva eats tapeworm eggs.

Segment dries and breaks to release eggs.

spray, burning with a cigarette end (not to be recommended for obvious reasons!) and removal by hand. The important thing to remember is that, once disturbed, the tick will lock its jaws into the animal and when you attempt to remove it, the head will break away from the body and be left in the animal. This area can then turn septic so, unless you are very skilled, it is unwise to remove ticks by hand. The best method we have found over the years is a small wire loop attached to a plastic handle which, when run across the animal's skin, lifts the tick, jaws and all, and tugs it out of the skin. This has proved highly successful and never leaves jaws behind even if you disturb the tick first, thus

causing it to lock its jaws. This item, is essential to anyone exercising dogs in tick-infested forests.

Removing a tick.

SKIN PROBLEMS

Siberian Huskies, if fed on a good-quality diet, rarely suffer from skin conditions and it is not a breed with a history of hereditary skin complaints.

ZINC DEFICIENCY

However, one problem which the Husky does suffer from, although the incidence is relatively low, is zinc deficiency. This appears to be a breed-related condition and usual symptoms are bare patches of skin and itchiness, particularly on the face. The problem is easily treated by the addition of zinc tablets to the diet and a skin treatment to reduce the irritation. Again, this is a condition to discuss with your vet.

WET ECZEMA

One other relatively common condition, particularly during the spring and summer moulting time, is wet eczema. It is usually caused by the dog chewing his skin as a result of coat loss. Any break in the skin will allow bacteria to enter and thus cause an infection or 'hot spot'. This can be easily treated but is best avoided by ensuring that your dog's coat is thoroughly combed out while moulting.

THE SIBERIAN BITCH
SEASONS

Siberian Huskies are still relatively close to their ancestry and therefore are quite 'basic' dogs. In addition they come from a cold and inhospitable climate with only a short time suitable for breeding in each year. As a result they quite commonly come into season only once a year, unlike dogs which have been domesticated for many, many generations and come into season twice a year. Having said that, seasons do vary from female to female, with some coming into season annually (or at even longer intervals) and others coming into season every five months. For those not planning to breed, the former is extremely convenient, but, for those waiting for a bitch to come into season in order to breed her, it can be very frustrating.

Siberians are easily cared for when in season. They tend to be very clean but bear in mind that there are 'panties' available for dogs which are very convenient and will keep your carpets from being marked. Just remember to take them off your bitch when you let her outside because they are easily forgotten since they hardly show. You should keep her separated from males for at least three weeks to be on the safe side and do not leave her unsupervised in the garden, as bitches in season can be a little more determined than usual to get out.

FALSE PREGNANCY

Most breeds of dog are commonly affected by false pregnancies and Siberians are certainly no exception. The bitch is 'programmed' to have puppies when she has been in season. Many bitches suffer from quite serious false pregnancies, their bodies believing that they have puppies to care for, lactating and altering both their character and their behaviour. This can be very distressing for any bitch and you should seriously consider having your bitch spayed if she is a constant sufferer. Discuss it with your vet though, as there are new products coming on the market all the time and he may have other suggestions.

NEUTERING

Neutering a Siberian should generally be considered as a last resort – to be carried out to resolve severe cases of false pregnancy for instance, rather than as a convenience or as a solution for behavioural problems such as inter-male aggression. While there are many reasons given for neutering, you should bear in mind that one of the main outcomes will be the ruination of your dog's coat. This is not something which most vets or behaviourists will warn you about, but consider it seriously. The overgrown and overthick coat that comes after neutering is extremely hard to look after and will certainly make running in harness a hotter business for the dog.

The only justifiable reason for neutering either sex (other than a medical one) is if this allows your household to live together more peacefully by avoiding seasons, but you should watch your timing since it is

Older bitches can fall victim to pyometra, a serious womb infection.

possible to 'lock' a bitch into a false pregnancy if she is spayed while this is going on. Discuss this carefully with your vet before proceeding.

PYOMETRA

Having warned against neutering, there are, however, certain circumstances where it is unavoidable and one of these is if your bitch develops a condition called pyometra. Pyometra is an infection of the womb. It is fairly common in older bitches and, when it occurs, it requires urgent surgery similar to a hysterectomy in humans. One of the most common signs is that the bitch drinks much more than usual. She may also have a raised temperature. Do not delay in obtaining veterinary help if you suspect this may be a problem. The operation is a major one and she will need time and care to get well again.

WHELPING PROBLEMS

Problems during whelping and post-whelping are uncommon in Siberians but if they do occur, as in any breed, they can be very serious. Immediate action is needed, so make yourself aware of the symptoms.

UTERINE INERTIA

Whelping is covered in the chapter on breeding but, to repeat the advice given, before the arrival of the first puppy it is inadvisable to allow your bitch to continue to have contractions for more than two hours without seeking veterinary advice. Similarly, if your bitch has been straining for more than an hour and a half between puppies or has been sitting about panting and in distress without straining, call the vet as there may be a problem with uterine inertia. Your vet will advise you but it is important not to simply leave her without taking any action. A Caesarean may be necessary to deliver the puppies. The majority of bitches accept their pups once they come around from the anaesthetic but you need to ensure that the puppies are dried and kept warm for the short time the mother is out of action. Suturing from the Caesarean does not seem to impede the pups or cause too much discomfort to the mother while feeding, but you should keep an extra-vigilant eye on her.

ECLAMPSIA

Post-whelping problems include eclampsia and mastitis. Eclampsia is caused by insufficient calcium. The symptoms of eclampsia (milk fever) are quite easy to spot: the bitch will be wobbly and disorientated and may wander about on unsteady feet. Get her to the vet immediately. While the symptoms are worrying, the problem is easily and speedily cured. Administration of calcium directly into the bloodstream quickly returns the bitch to normal. The condition will be avoided by feeding a good-quality complete food. Do not be tempted to add calcium supplements to the diet if it is already complete, as this can cause problems in itself.

MASTITIS

Mastitis may occur at any stage of lactation. It makes the bitch feel very miserable with a high temperature and a reddened, swollen milk gland or glands. Antibiotic treatment is needed and the pups should be removed and hand-fed while the infection is treated.

HEREDITARY CONDITIONS

Siberians are a pretty healthy breed but, like the vast majority of breeds, they do have inherited conditions just as humans do. It is possible to carry out genetic screening for carriers of hereditary diseases, and thus avoid using these dogs in our breeding programmes. These tests are not yet available for conditions of the Siberian Husky. In the meantime it is essential to use all the health schemes available to us to maintain and improve the health of our breed.

The Siberian Husky is a healthy, robust breed, but it does have some hereditary problems.

EYE PROBLEMS

Eye problems are probably the most common inherited condition in Siberians. Hereditary glaucoma, cataracts, persistent pupillary membrane, progressive retinal atrophy and retinal dystrophy have all been identified. The most serious of these is glaucoma. All Siberians should be tested for this disease prior to breeding and any dog identified as being predisposed to the disease must not be bred from. The resulting condition is extremely painful for the dog – just as it is in humans – and must be avoided at all costs. The other conditions are less serious and, while it would be unwise to breed from a dog affected with cataracts, breeding from siblings may be necessary in order to retain other desired characteristics. If and when genetic screening is available, we will be able to identify carriers and exclude these dogs from breeding as well.

For the time being, annual physical screening is recommended to identify those dogs which are affected, as many of these diseases can appear later in life.

HIPS AND ELBOWS

Hip dysplasia can be an inherited condition and is common in certain breeds. In essence, this is a poorly formed hip joint that may result in dislocation and osteoarthritic changes which are very painful. Dogs that suffer from hip dysplasia can have limited movement and a resulting poor quality of life, so the condition should be avoided at all costs. Siberian Huskies generally have very good hips, but hip X-rays should be taken of those dogs that are intended to be bred from, both sire and dam, in order to maintain low scores and the health of our breed in which free movement is so essential.

Elbow joint screening is also available, although, as with hips, inherited problems in this joint have not been identified in the Siberian. However, in view of the fact that the schemes are intended to be preventative, it may be wise to discuss the use of this scheme with your vet.

ZINC DEFICIENCY

Zinc deficiency has already been covered in the section on skin conditions and, although this is a relatively rare problem in Siberians, it does appear to be an inherited condition. Since it can be distressing for the animal affected it would be worthwhile to out-cross to an unrelated line if you have identified this problem in your Siberians.

LIVER SHUNT

Liver shunt is an inherited problem that can be lethal. The blood supply to the liver is incorrectly formed and the liver cannot function properly. The malformation may be outside the liver or within the liver itself. In some cases, surgery may rectify the situation but, in more severe cases, this is not possible and the dog may have to be put to sleep. However, the condition *may* be managed through diet and the administration of medicines but the success of this depends on the seriousness of the problem in a particular individual.

Early signs of thyroid deficiency are lethargy and poor condition.

Liver shunt is recognised as a hereditary problem in a number of breeds but appears to have a very low occurrence in Siberian Huskies – possibly limited to particular lines. The low incidence, while fortunate in one way, also makes identification of carriers and eradication of the problem even more difficult. Until genetic identification of carriers is possible, it is important to identify and report affected lines in order to ensure that the problem does not increase.

THYROID DEFICIENCY

Thyroid deficiency is also an inherited condition and occurs relatively commonly in Siberians. Symptoms are many and varied but the most common early sign is that the dog becomes lethargic and lacks his usual energy. Poor coat quality, infertility and generally low condition are all signs of the possibility of low thyroid levels in the Siberian.

The condition is identified through a blood test and is rectified through daily oral drug administration. Without this, the animal's quality of life is poor and the condition will eventually lead to death. With treatment, the Siberian can be expected to live a normal, healthy life. If you suspect that your dog may be suffering from hypothyroidism, let your vet know that the condition is hereditary in Siberians. He can then rule the condition in or out early on in the process of diagnosis, rather than looking for a 'needle in a haystack'.

INFERTILITY

Infertility is not a common problem in Siberians since they are still a very natural breed and, by definition, infertility is hard to pass on to the next generation!

MONORCHIDISM AND CRYPTORCHIDISM

Far more common is the problem of cryptorchidism. To explain the terms: monorchidism is the term applied to a dog which only has one testicle; the other testicle is simply not present, either descended into the scrotum or retained in the abdomen. Bilateral cryptorchidism applies when both testicles are present but not descended into the scrotum. Unilateral cryptorchidism means that only one testicle is descended and the other is retained in the abdomen.

Your vet may be able to identify a retained testicle. A cryptorchid should be checked by your vet at about a year old since there is an increased risk of testicular cancer in retained testicles. Regular annual health checks are advisable for all dogs and this will include checking for any sign of unusual growth. Many vets recommend routine removal of retained testicles, and most will castrate the dog at the same time.

However you should consider this carefully before going ahead with castration. The dog's coat growth, in both males and females, is largely hormonally controlled. Castration and spaying removes that control, which can prove disastrous in a heavy-coated breed

A long-coated Siberian should be left entire if at all possible, to prevent the coat becoming even heavier.

such as the Siberian. If one testicle is descended, you can ask your vet to remove only the retained one since the descended testicle will still produce the hormones that the dog requires for normal coat control. This is particularly important in a dog that is being exercised heavily and absolutely essential in a long-coated Siberian.

While on the subject of castration, you should also be wary of 'behaviourists' who advocate this as a means of subduing dominant behaviour. It is rarely effective.

VACCINATIONS

Vaccination is a controversial subject. The one thing that is certain is that the lack of highly contagious, killer diseases affecting dogs nowadays is almost entirely due to effective vaccination campaigns. While there will always be individual dogs who have never been vaccinated and yet live long and healthy lives, this is clearly aided by the fact that dogs around them have been vaccinated and therefore the particular dog is never faced with the disease. Most owners will at least have their puppy's first course of vaccination completed. Whether they continue annually is a matter for the individual and the veterinary practice. A number of practices are now recommending vaccination every three years and blood tests to check immunity levels in between.

In some countries and states, rabies vaccination in particular is compulsory and must be administered regularly. The relaxing of UK quarantine laws allows dogs to travel to some overseas countries, providing certain conditions of identification and vaccination are fulfilled. Rabies vaccination is required for all dogs entering the UK and boosters in the UK are necessary every two years.

In the US, vaccinations are also available for such conditions as the tick-borne Lyme disease but use of this varies from state to state. Consult your vet as to which vaccinations are necessary for your dog in the area in which you are living.

SUNBURN AND HEAT STRESS

It may sound odd, but Siberian Huskies love heat! They will lie in front of the fire on winter evenings and out in the sun in the summer, so it is up to you to regulate their heat intake and to ensure that they do not get sunburnt. White dogs in particular are vulnerable to sunburn as their skin has little pigment to protect itself. The most vulnerable areas are the ears and if you look at white-coated ears in the sunshine you will see the sun shining through them, damaging the skin and with the potential to cause skin

cancer. This is relatively common in cats nowadays, so do not dismiss the possibility. Using sun block on the dog's ears is well worthwhile if applied every couple of days, and encourage your dogs to come into the shade if they have been lying out for too long. Make sure that you provide sufficient shade in the garden or run and check at all times of day. The simple attachment of a blanket or sheet to the wire of the run using pegs, can provide good shade.

While sunburn is a serious risk, heat stress can be lethal. Heatstroke can occur at any time of year, as a result of overheating in a vehicle, of running in too high a temperature or just from allowing dogs to overdo exercise. During heat stress, excessive panting can cause over-ventilation leading to high losses of carbon dioxide from the blood. The blood becomes too alkaline and upsets the overall metabolism. Once a dog collapses, even though he may appear to

The lack of pigment in white dogs makes them prone to sunburn and skin cancer.

Siberians are renowned for chewing their feet.

recover, he is likely to have serious, long-term brain damage. When running dogs in the summer, even at the coolest time of day, stop and water your dogs regularly, if only to check that they are not overdoing things. Really keen dogs, particularly large ones, are a risk to themselves, as they will do too much before they realise the effects. Look out for heavy, noisy panting or a deep red-coloured tongue, which may even start to turn blue. Adding electrolyte replacement products (usually sold in powder form) to the drinking water helps to replace lost body fluids and salts more quickly and to restore normal metabolism.

Obviously, no dog should be left in a car in hot weather. Dogs have a higher body temperature than our own so it takes less time for them to reach a dangerously high temperature. Leaving windows open and the car in the shade is not enough to guard against problems – the sun moves round and open windows do not guarantee movement of air through the car.

Cooling the dog (internally and externally) is critical, since dogs have so little exposed area from which to sweat. Immersing the dog in cool (not cold) water and getting it to drink will aid recovery but you should obtain veterinary help immediately if you suspect that your dog may be suffering from heatstroke.

CHEWING FEET

Chewing of feet and wrists is a common habit in Siberians. They are dogs that are particularly conscious of their feet and do not generally like their feet being handled. However, some of them will sit for hours licking or chewing the top of their front paws. Once you have satisfied yourself that there is no cut, scratch or other damage that might be causing a sudden interest in a particular foot, this is not something to worry about. Bitches will do this in particular if they have a false pregnancy. It appears that their feet become their 'puppies' and receive all the licking which pups would otherwise have been given. In females at other times and in males, it appears simply to be a habit. Chewing often results in very short fur on top of the knuckles and wrist but does not cause any other harm, so should be ignored. There appears to be a certain hereditary element to this behaviour since it is often noted in offspring which have moved on to other homes and therefore could not have learnt it by copying.

INTESTINAL DISORDERS
DIARRHOEA AND VOMITING

Siberian Huskies, in common with a number of breeds, have somewhat sensitive digestive systems. It is a fact of

Siberian lore that chewing gum or other rubbish gleaned from the pavement, and filthy water drunk from a puddle, appear to cause little or no upset, while good food specially prepared and provided for your dog may cause diarrhoea unless carefully chosen. Top-quality extruded (kibbled) complete dry dog foods seem to suit the Siberian best. A little fresh or canned meat may be added for variety but, essentially, all the nutrients are already present and this is unnecessary except for our own feeling of providing an interesting diet for our dogs. The addition of hot or warm water just before serving is recommended and this will generally keep your dog healthy.

Overfeeding is another common cause of food-related diarrhoea. Feed below the recommended quantity to begin with and build up gradually so you can identify the point at which problems may arise. The dog's digestive system does not include the enzymes needed to digest raw starch, so low-cost, flake-type foods should be avoided. These may well cause upsets and, in any case, more food is required to compensate for the amount of indigestible material fed.

Vomiting and diarrhoea caused by infection will occur in any dog just as it does in humans. A quick trip to the vet is recommended for your own peace of mind, even though, very often, the problem will cure itself. However, a particularly nasty attack may require treatment with antibiotics and fluids, so it is worth a prompt call to the vet. Beware, though, the vet that recommends a different diet to get the dog back on the mend. It is better simply not to feed for 24 hours than to give a different food which may well lead to diarrhoea for a different reason in the Siberian!

Vomiting and diarrhoea may also be caused by some form of poisoning if your Siberian is in the habit of rooting around in things he should not touch. This is a particular danger for puppies who do not have the same awareness that adults appear to develop of what is and is not good for them. If you suspect your Siberian may have eaten something toxic, call your vet immediately.

BLOAT

Bloat or gastric torsion is uncommon in Siberians. There are many theories put forward as to the cause of bloat but there is certainly a breed-associated element and, fortunately, it does not arise often in the Siberian. Sensible feeding and exercise regimes are recommended to reduce the possibility of bloat occurring. Feeding two small meals a day rather than one large one, restricting exercise immediately after feeding and encouraging dogs to eat more slowly are all suggested. The latter may be achieved by adding a couple of large balls or stones (more than three inches in diameter) to the food bowl, forcing the dog to eat round them rather than gulping his food.

8 BREEDING AND REARING A LITTER

The old idea that every bitch should have a litter, and that it is good for her to do so, has now been exposed as utter rubbish. You should only plan a litter if you wish to keep at least one of the offspring and you are seriously committed to the breed and its future. *Never* plan to have a litter just to have puppies to sell. Whether you are an experienced breeder or a novice, this is irresponsible profiteering. It simply brings more dogs into the world with the attendant risks to their happy future, particularly in a specialist breed like the Siberian Husky.

We all believe we give our dogs the best home and, if you are a caring person, you will soon discover how worrying it can be to sell pups. No matter how secure the new home appears, couples separate, babies arrive, jobs change, circumstances alter. And, no matter how much you have explained to potential owners about the breed, there will be those who say they

understand, and accept that their dog will never be allowed to run free, and then ignore all your warnings.

IS YOUR BITCH SUITABLE?
If you wish to breed, you should ensure that your bitch is the best possible example of the breed before you begin. The temptation to breed from your first pet bitch is enormous since you love her dearly and, to you, she will always be the best. But remember, if you are planning to continue in the breed – and even if you are just planning one litter you will find that things change before you know it – your first breeding will form the basis for your future in the breed. This is true whether you are planning to work or to show your dogs or simply want them as companions, and is important no matter what your plans.

So try to compare your bitch with other Siberians. Being objective about your own dog is difficult and, if you cannot do it honestly, then talk to other people – judges, other owners, her breeder – and be prepared to take the criticisms; then you can make an informed judgement on her suitability, or otherwise, for breeding.

If you are working your dog and want to breed for your own team, then the most important consideration must be your bitch's attitude to running in harness. Without this, you are wasting your time in thinking of breeding from her. Even if you only have one Siberian, you will have joined up with others to harness-train her, and will know how keen she is to work. If she is half-hearted, or just goes along with the

Your bitch should be an excellent example of the breed before you even consider having pups from her.

whole business, then start again with a bitch from proven working lines. If she is truly keen, then go ahead, providing you have checked out the other important considerations such as good temperament and good conformation.

Whatever your reason for breeding, you will be able to assess certain things for yourself and, among these, temperament is the most important. The Siberian Husky is an easy-going, gentle dog with a somewhat reserved nature. If your dog does not match up to this, then do not breed. Many breeds have been ruined by people trying to make a fast buck from that breed's growing popularity without worrying about temperament. They have, consequently, bred dogs which have proved to have less than suitable natures for living with people. I have not yet met a 'nasty' Siberian, but it could happen, and keeping a watchful eye on temperament is important.

CHOOSING A STUD DOG

This can be one of the most difficult decisions to make. We all agonise over the possibilities, especially when there are a number of suitable dogs available. If you show or work your dog, you will be aware which males are considered to be the top performers. In this working breed, the prime consideration must be whether or not the dog runs well and has working attitude. These traits can quickly be lost from our breed if we do not give them due prominence in our

The stud dog should have an impeccable temperament.

breeding plans. The Standard for the Siberian Husky does not worry about coat colour and eye colour, so these do not need to be considered when choosing a suitable mate. This leaves you able to concentrate on conformation, movement, temperament and overall type, along with working attitude.

HEALTH CONSIDERATIONS

Also important are health considerations. Discussed earlier are hereditary conditions of the Siberian such as glaucoma, cataracts and bilateral cryptorchidism. Clearly, no one should consider breeding from a dog or bitch that has primary glaucoma or is predisposed to the disease. Advice from veterinary specialists is that all dogs affected with, for instance, hereditary cataracts, plus all their siblings and their parents, should be excluded from future breedings. In a perfect world this would be the ideal, but in many cases this would exclude some excellent dogs, so the pros and cons have to be weighed

up. It is therefore of prime importance to discuss the suitability of a particular male and female with breed specialists, before going ahead. Line breeding is a very good way of fixing certain traits in your dogs, but it can also be important to out-cross now and again in order to avoid hereditary disease.

In the relatively near future, it is hoped that genetic tests will be available to identify carriers of particular conditions in the Siberian, and this will make it much easier to exclude carriers while using their littermates who have been shown not to carry the genes for a particular disease. In the meantime, the best course to follow is to discuss the possibilities with knowledgeable people in the breed and only go ahead when you are sure you have made the best choice. Never use 'the dog down the road' simply because he is the closest!

TIMING THE MATING

The majority of stud dog owners prefer to have bitches brought to them. The dog is more relaxed on his own territory and does not need to spend the first half an hour getting to know his surroundings as well as his new friend. Most people take their bitches to dogs too early. We all suffer from impatience and this is understandable, but it is distressing and frustrating for both dog and bitch if she is not ready. Twelve to fourteen days into the season is generally early enough and some bitches may not be ready until 20 days or longer.

SECOND MATINGS

Most people prefer to have two matings, but it is worth allowing your bitch to do the deciding. If she is willing to be mated a second time then all well and good, but if she is definitely against the idea, it may mean that she has already 'taken' and you should not push the issue. In any case there is no point in mating again within 48 hours, as sperm remains active for that length of time. When you take your bitch home, see how she reacts to other dogs over the next few days and, if she still seems keen, take her back to be mated again. Use her instincts: no textbook can better them.

THE MATING

The owner of the stud dog will generally supervise the mating but will ask you to hold your bitch once the dogs have tied; a wriggling female at this point can be difficult for a male to deal with, especially a young, inexperienced one, so it is helpful to steady her. Apart from this, Siberians should be allowed to get on with things on their own. Supervise by all means, since the dogs generally do not know each other, but otherwise let them do their own thing. Why people have to become involved to the extent that they do in some breeds is beyond understanding!

The tie may last from a few minutes to 20 or 30 – tiring for everyone in the latter case but, once they separate, it remains only for you to praise everyone, allow them to have a quick 'clean-up' and travel home. Return a couple of days later if this is practicable, but bear in mind the earlier points.

REGISTRATION FORMS

It is the responsibility of the stud dog owner to complete the Kennel Club Registration Form at the time of mating and to give it to you before you leave – generally after you have paid for the stud dog's services. This form is the record of the mating and is essential when the time comes to register the litter and their names.

THE PREGNANT BITCH

Now begins the long wait. Nine weeks can pass very slowly when you are looking forward to the arrival of your litter, but there is no reason to treat your bitch much differently from usual. Increasing her food in the last couple of weeks, by about 20 per cent, is advisable for any bitch who is on the slim side, particularly if she is not a good eater under normal circumstances. If you work your dogs, you can continue to run her in a medium-slow team. Some people withdraw them from work completely, others continue up until five weeks into the pregnancy. When you stop working her, make sure she still gets exercise on the lead – few Siberians like to be total 'couch potatoes' and, if you continue to keep her exercised, it will be much easier to get her back into training once the puppies are reared.

Keep a close eye on your pregnant bitch, so that you can adapt her lifestyle.

You can have your bitch scanned from three weeks into the pregnancy which will let you know, fairly accurately, how many puppies are expected. Or you can wait and see. If you do not think she is pregnant, it is still advisable to keep an eye on her around the time the puppies would be due. Siberians have a happy knack of carrying the odd puppy well hidden away and then producing one just when you were certain none were due!

PREPARATIONS FOR WHELPING
Most bitches go off their food about 24 hours before whelping. You should prepare an area for her to have her pups and where she can stay for the first three weeks or so. Different types of whelping box are available. The old-fashioned ones with railings are still much favoured, as puppies can lie behind their mother without being squashed, enabling them

to crawl out and find her. Even the most attentive of mothers may be unaware of a puppy hidden behind her and the puppy can get cold and die within a few hours if undetected.

Covered whelping boxes are generally favoured by the bitch but do make it more difficult to supervise from the human point of view. The advantage to this type of box is that warmth is retained more effectively. In either case, it is advisable to keep the room warm, or suspend a heat lamp above an area of the box. While the bitch may find this too warm, the puppies have little ability to maintain body heat and need the extra warmth even in warm weather.

Having set up the room, let the bitch get accustomed to it, particularly if it is in an area of the house to which she does not usually have access. It is important that she is secure from other pets, but not so cut off that the puppies will not hear household noises as they grow. A utility room or even a large cupboard in the kitchen (with the door open!) would be suitable. Most bitches will want to choose their own spot to have their puppies. However, this is usually the most inconvenient or unsuitable place (in your view!) so you may need to insist on your choice. A frantic period of digging at the floor or base of the whelping box usually precedes the arrival of the puppies so it is a good idea to provide newspaper to allow her to fulfil her nesting instincts. Order can be restored once the puppies arrive!

You should also have on hand a cardboard box with a warm hot-water bottle (or heated pad) in the bottom, covered with a small towel or blanket, which you can use to place puppies in while other puppies arrive. A pair of curved-ended scissors are a good idea plus a good canine milk supplement and feeding bottle or plastic syringe, just in case.

THE WHELPING
Once the puppies start to arrive, you will be kept busy. Siberians are very instinct-driven and will get on with things happily on their own, but it is still worthwhile to help out, particularly with a first litter. As each puppy arrives, you should ensure that the airway is clear by removing the embryonic sac across his mouth and face. At this stage, the puppy is still attached by the umbilical cord to the placenta and the bitch will bite through the cord and eat the placenta. The placenta is full of nutrients, and allowing her to swallow a few is okay but, if you can retrieve some, then do; the results of ingesting a lot of placentas can be pretty dire for the digestive system. You may need to help with detaching the puppy by using the scissors to cut through the cord. If you need to do so, cut at least four inches down the cord away from the puppy's abdomen. The resulting cord will shrivel up and detach from the puppy within the next 24 hours or so.

Puppies arrive at varying intervals, with sometimes just 15 minutes between them and sometimes up to two hours. If your bitch has been straining for more than an hour and a half without producing another puppy, call the vet as there may be a problem. Your vet will advise you, but it is important not to simply leave her straining without taking any action. Similarly, before the arrival of the first puppy, it is inadvisable to allow your bitch to strain for more than two hours without seeking veterinary advice.

You can help out with drying puppies using a soft, clean towel, but allow the bitch to do most of the cleaning. It is important for her to bond with the puppies and she may not appreciate too much interference. However, the majority of Siberians are easy-going, although very attentive, mothers and take to motherhood like a duck to water.

It is important to ensure that mum goes outside to relieve herself at some point as she will be busy concentrating on her puppies and may not want to leave them. Put her on a collar and lead to take her out so that you can watch and ensure that another puppy does not appear in the garden – not an unknown occurrence!

POST-WHELPING
Once all the litter has arrived, change the bedding, putting down clean newspaper and a clean piece of nylon fur. This latter is essential since it gives the puppies some grip so they can reach mum and hang on while they are feeding, and it also keeps

Two-week-old pups. At this stage, a week prior to weaning, there is surprisingly little for the breeder to do.

them warm. Puppies can get about remarkably well even when newly born, but they need a surface that they can grip, not just newspaper. It is advisable to ask your vet to call round at this point to check both the mother and the puppies, to ensure that she has indeed produced all the puppies, has no retained placentas and to make sure the pups are all healthy.

After that there is very little for you to do, except watch the puppies grow, until it is time to wean them. Most people weigh their puppies daily for the first week and once or twice a week after that. You should expect a drop in weight the day after the puppies are born, since the bitch's milk does not start to flow properly until 24 hours after the puppies first start to suckle. This is perfectly normal but after that a steady increase will be seen.

WEANING

Once the puppies reach three weeks old, you should begin weaning. You may need to start earlier if it is a large litter or if one or two of the pups are not gaining weight as consistently as the others. Breeders recommend all manner of foods for puppies but the simplest and most reliable are, undoubtedly, complete puppy foods.

Choose a top-quality food and soak it to form a paste. Place a little in each pup's mouth and give him or her a chance to get the taste. It will not be long before they are charging at the bowl and demanding as much food as you are willing to provide (or their waistlines dictate!). Once they have all had a little food, give them back to mum and let her feed and wash them. Involving the bitch in the process will ensure that she does not become anxious, although in some cases it may be necessary to separate her from them while feeding in order to ensure that it is the puppies that eat the food, not mum.

Increase the amount of food given at each meal until you have reached the amount recommended for the age group by the food manufacturer. This amount should be split into four meals. The number of meals will be reduced to three at 12 weeks old, and two at 6 months. The main cause of diarrhoea at

120

this age is overfeeding so, if this happens, reduce the amount of food and take the increases more slowly.

It is best to recommend to new owners that, even when their pups become adults, they should be fed twice a day and not cut to one meal. Two meals mean that the amount to be consumed at one time is halved. It is better for the digestive system since it is not overloaded and it also makes life much more interesting for the dog. After all, we would not want to eat all our food in one meal each day so why should our canine friends?

Pups feeding on solids at three weeks of age.

WORMING

In the areas of both worming and vaccination, opinions vary from vet to vet and you should consult with your practice to see which worming products they recommend and at what age they vaccinate puppies. Suffice to say that pretty well all puppies have worms,

which have been passed from their mother in her milk, and it is essential to treat them regularly in the first few weeks of life.

While mum is still cleaning up after the puppies, a cycle is set up so that worm eggs are ingested by the mother, reinfecting her, and conveyed to the puppies through her milk, thus reinfecting them. Breaking the cycle can be particularly difficult if the puppies

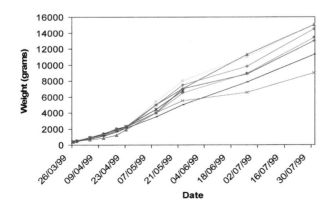

Puppy Growth Chart

Chile
Kite
Breeze
Rufus
Jana
Kheta
Suki
Nyssa

The growth rates of a typical litter of Siberian Husky pups.

start to copy their mother and start cleaning up after each other too – this is very common and leads to behaviour which we find revolting but is entirely normal to the dog. Most owners whose dogs eat faeces are too embarrassed to admit it and as a result never realise just how common this is. Youngsters sometimes grow out of the habit but many continue into adulthood. Either way, do not worry about it; it may be unpleasant for us but the dog does not see things the same way!

It is generally recommended that worming treatment is given at four, six and eight weeks (worming mum at the same time is important while the pups are still suckling) and then at monthly intervals to six months. After that, adults should be wormed twice a year. Worming treatments come in different forms: tablets, pastes and syrups, and the easiest of these to administer, particularly to young puppies, is the syrup. Follow the directions given by your vet or on the pack and keep a record so you know what you did and when. That way you will not overdose or under-dose the pups.

VACCINATIONS

Vaccination is a controversial subject. The one thing that is certain is that the lack of highly contagious, killer diseases affecting dogs nowadays is almost entirely due to effective vaccination campaigns. Most owners will at least have their puppy's first course of vaccination completed.

Whether they continue annually is a matter for the individual and the veterinary practice. As stated in the chapter on health, a number of practices are now recommending vaccination every three years and blood tests to check immunity levels in between.

EARLY SOCIALISATION

The first vaccinations are usually given at eight or nine weeks with the second following between two and three weeks later. After a further two weeks has elapsed, the pups are ready for the big wide world! However, there is a major drawback to this schedule. If strictly adhered to, it means that puppies may not be out and about until they are

A pup should be socialised from as early as three weeks.

nearly four months old and this can have serious consequences for their socialisation and confidence. It is therefore important that both the breeder and the new owner socialise the puppies as much as possible. Before three weeks of age, it is best not to disturb the mother and puppies but, once weaned, the pups should meet as many new people, and hear as many new sounds as possible. Playing the radio and running the vacuum cleaner and washing machine nearby are all good training for the pup's new life, so make sure you carry out this essential part of puppy rearing.

REGISTRATION

Using the form that the stud dog owner completed and gave you at the time of mating, you can register the puppies with the appropriate kennel club. You will need to have names, and alternatives, for the litter and complete the form which asks for details of the parents, the colour and sex of the puppies, date of birth etc. This form should be sent off, with the appropriate fee, as early as possible in order to ensure that you have the registration documents to hand when the puppies go to their new homes. Remember that you will also need to supply a copy of each puppy's pedigree when the new owners come to collect. You can either write the pedigree out yourself or obtain a printed copy from your national kennel club.

A word at this point about other documentation: many breeders like to ask new owners to sign a contract. This ensures that everyone understands their undertaking and is left in no doubt about any verbal agreements that may have been made. We include reference to any endorsements which may have been placed on the puppy's registration and state that, if the new owners are in any doubt about their ability to keep the puppy or dog at any time in the future, they are obliged to return it to us for rehoming. Other items may be included but you should make it clear to the new owners just what you are asking them to agree to and give them a copy of the contract as well as retaining one for your own records. We find this an invaluable exercise and anyone unwilling to sign up to your conditions (as long as they are reasonable) is not going to be the right owner for your puppies.

INSURANCE

Free insurance cover for the first six weeks after the puppy leaves the breeder is available from a number of specialist pet insurance companies and is well worth providing for your pups. For any household with one or two pets, veterinary insurance is a sensible and worthwhile proposition. For a relatively small premium, owners are protected from the possibility of large veterinary bills and, even for the breeder, it is worth considering, as the cost of a

Caesarean can be high. For multiple dog-owning households though, the currently available policies generally do not make economic sense since the premiums far outweigh any benefits which might come from cover.

You should take a look at the policies available for yourself and for the new owners and see which ones best suit your needs and those of the new puppy-owning household, bearing in mind that some policies also cover damage caused by puppies in their new homes.

FINDING SUITABLE HOMES

And now comes the most difficult part. The Siberian Husky is not an ideal pet for everyone. New owners have to be dedicated to the breed and must be warned against letting the dog off the lead and the possibility of chasing livestock – just as you were when you bought your first Siberian. It is therefore essential that you meet prospective new owners and that they fully understand the commitment they are taking on.

In many ways, it is better to sell to other Siberian owners since they already understand the breed. However, unless people know you and are looking for your particular breeding, they may not be interested in your litter. The other problem with selling to current owners is that you obviously want your puppies to be loved and wanted as pets first and foremost; the attitude of some owners (in many breeds, not just Siberians) can be that they are more interested in a dog's show and work abilities than in their companionship, particularly if they already have a lot of dogs.

Advertising in the dog press, through puppy agencies and even in the local paper can be good sources of new homes, but word of mouth is often the most effective.

In all cases be wary: check, check and check again. This is a specialist breed and must not be sold to those who are simply buying on 'looks'. Siberians look wonderful on the end of the lead but most people get fed up with being dragged around the park and being

There are queues of people wanting Siberians, but not all of them are suitable owners for this demanding breed.

unable to let the dog loose; they also get tired of having their garden dug over and of having small dogs and cats threatened. Be prepared for failures. Even the best-chosen home can turn out to be a problem. Divorce, redundancy etc. can happen to anyone and your pup may be the loser. You should always be prepared to take back any puppy or adult that you bred. Rescue societies are not best placed for rehoming Siberians and specialist breed rescue is always hard-pressed.

DEPARTURE DAY

When the new owners come to collect, sit down quietly with them, away from the puppies, to go through all the paperwork that needs sorting out. You should provide the new owners with the signed Registration Transfer form, completed pedigree and, preferably, insurance cover. Give them a receipt for their money and, if you are asking them to sign a contract, then this should be signed now. You should go through your written feeding and care recommendations and ensure they are happy with everything. When all this is done, you can relax and go to the pups. Items to give to new owners:

- Pedigree
- Insurance cover note
- Registration document
- Receipt
- Contract
- Feeding & general care instructions
- Sample of food.

On the day that a puppy is due to go to

Saying goodbye to the pups can be emotional – but it can also be a relief!

his new home, and depending on when the owners are coming to collect and how long the journey is, it is best not to feed beforehand as it is more than likely that this will lead to travel sickness. You should advise the new owners to bring with them a blanket or 'fluffy' for the puppy. This can then be played with by the littermates and will smell familiar when the pup is on his own. A travel box is advisable so the puppy can sleep on the journey. If you have had a chance to take the litter of puppies out in the car a few times (just around the block is enough), then so much the better, since the pups will be used to the noise of a car and will not have to cope with too many new experiences at once.

Most new owners want to carry their new pup home on their laps, which is very understandable but, if they want to do this, then suggest they travel in the back of the car along with the travel box so they can contain the puppy if he gets too wriggly or needs to get some sleep. Certainly, if the puppy is being collected by one person, you must insist that a suitable crate is provided and the puppy travels in it. Siberians are generally good travellers and the more they become accustomed to travelling by car in their early days, the better.

A quick phone call when they arrive home will put your mind at rest, but then it is probably best to leave them alone for a few days while everyone settles in together. As long as the new owners know they can reach you at any time for advice and a listening ear, they will feel confident and all should go well.

RESCUE AND REHOMING

The subject of rescue has already been touched upon but it is worth spending a little time considering, since the number of Siberians needing to be rehomed is steadily increasing as the breed grows in popularity.

For many people, a rescued Siberian is an ideal choice. House-training and puppy care are time-consuming and an adult may well fit in easily to a new home. If you have children and other pets, make sure that the rescue dog has already been accustomed to these, as it is far less easy to train an adult than a puppy to accept crawling and clutching babies, and other pets.

Siberians have a relatively large rescue problem for the size of the breed, for two reasons. Firstly, because new owners do not fully realise what they are taking on and/or breeders take insufficient care in placing their puppies. The second reason is that multiple-Siberian-owning households are relatively common in the breed and, when one of these falls apart, a lot of dogs need rehoming at the same time. If you have prospective owners who are unsure about taking on a puppy but seem to be the right type of person to have a Siberian, it may be a good idea to direct them towards a rescue dog.

Rescue Siberians are rarely problem dogs since the reasons for giving them up are more usually as given above, and they are very often more affectionate than the average, reserved adult Siberian, being only too pleased to have found their way into a new and loving home. They are therefore a good choice for the right owners and can be recommended.

INTRODUCTIONS TO THE PACK

If any of the dogs you bred need to be rehomed you should be prepared to take them back, or at least pay for their keep in rescue, while looking for a suitable new home. If you are of a mind to keep the dog, introducing him to the adult pack can be done relatively easily, providing this is handled carefully and over a period, although this does depend one the size and nature of your pack.

It is often best to make slightly 'sideways' introductions rather than direct ones. To explain: take the dogs out for a walk together when everyone is thinking of things other than the strange dog;

Dominance is being displayed towards the pup who is (sensibly) grovelling!

More grovelling – submission is critical in order to avoid aggression from adults in the pack.

travel in a vehicle with separate pens so the dogs can meet but not touch etc. This takes the sting out of the initial introduction. You can then supervise at home – ideally giving the new dog a cage to retreat to if the rest of the pack becomes a nuisance. Never leave the strange dog alone with the rest of the pack, no matter how relaxed they may seem together, until a few weeks have gone by and you are absolutely certain that there is no tension between any pack members and/or the new dog. This applies equally when introducing a new puppy to the pack but is even more important, since a puppy can very easily be killed by an overexcited and attacking mob. An adult does at least have size on his side. Whether adult or puppy, always err on the side of caution when introducing new members to an established pack.

9 SIBERIAN HUSKIES IN THE UK

The Siberian Husky is undoubtedly set to become a hugely popular breed in the UK – since it has grown from a small base to relatively large numbers in only thirty-odd years. The first Siberians of recent times to be imported came through the temporary posting of US service personnel and their families to the UK, some of whom bought their family pets with them to live 'on base'.

The first Siberian to be registered by the Kennel Club was as recently as 1969. She was a grey and white bitch with brown eyes called Yeso Pac's Tasha owned by Bill and Jean Cracknell. Bill was an American serviceman and Tasha travelled to Britain and did her stint in quarantine.

Tasha carried the important New England strains of Monadnock, Alyeska, Igloo Pak and, of course, Yeso Pac. The Cracknells also imported a black and white male from Anna Mae Forsberg, Savdajaures Samovar, whose arrival unfortunately coincided with a rabies

Kenstaff Sascha, daughter of one of the original Siberians, imported by the Profitts in the late 1960s.

scare, which resulted in the dog having an extended stay of eleven months in quarantine, rather than the usual six months.

Prior to that first registration, an English couple – Mr and Mrs Profitt – had seen Siberians when on holiday in Switzerland. They were attracted to the

128

Ch. Forstal's Mikishar the Amarok (driver's view of left lead), the first male UK Champion.

breed and imported, in 1968, a bitch named Togli who was dark grey, white and tan, and a silver grey male named Killik from the kennels of Helge and Benedict Ingstad in Norway. Togli was mainly from Seppala lineage along with Alaskan Anadyr lines. Her relationship to today's pedigrees can be traced back through Kenstaff Natasha and Kenstaff Sascha, litter sisters, bred by the Profitts from Togli and Ilya of Northwood, and owned by Mrs Liz Leich and Mrs Christine Jackson.

Returning from the US in 1971, Don and Liz Leich had brought with them Ilya and Douschka of Northwood. Despite the fact that they shared the same Northwood affix, the dogs were unrelated. In 1972, Douschka produced the first Forstal litter with Savdajaures Samovar, and one of the puppies, Sernik, was the first red Siberian in the UK.

FIRST MALE SHOW CHAMPION

Since these early introductions, there have been many imports from the United States, Canada and Europe in particular, as well as from other countries. Many have come from successful working kennels, as the enthusiasm of Don and

Liz Leich for running their dogs in harness and using them as they were intended spread to others and fuelled the need for proven working strains.

Micnicroc's Nanuska (Savdajaures Samovar ex Yeso Pac's Tasha) a grey and white bitch, was the dam of Forstal's Mikishar the Amarok, known as Miki, who became the first male Show Champion in the UK when he was nearly eleven years old, at the time when Champion status had just been awarded to the breed. Nanuska was one of a litter of seven, bred by the Cracknells in 1971.

One of Ilya and Douschka's pups was Forstal's Kassan, the black and white sire of Miki. Miki, who was a grey and white, was the sire of three Forstal Champions: Deki, another grey and white, whose dam was Forstal Roy-a-lin Zarnetsa, a piebald; Meshka, another grey and white, whose dam was Ch. Forstal Kooshak also a piebald; and Chutki, a black and white, whose dam was Roy-A-Lin's Apatchy Girl of Forstal, another piebald imported from Linda Arnett in the United States.

As well as being a Show Champion, Miki was an important lead dog for Forstal, helping to train many youngsters along the way.

ARRIVALS FROM HOLLAND

In 1981, there were two important arrivals from Holland to the Forstal kennel. Known to come from excellent working dogs, they were Goosack of Kolyma, a black and white dog (Alaskan's Pala of Anadyr ex Oleta of

Kolyma) and Green Beret's Snowy Lyscha, a grey and white bitch (Alaskan's Unik Knik of Anadyr ex Stanawoi's Siwaga). These two were descendents of Alaskan Anadyr lineage, Lyscha's grandsire being Alaskan's Nicolai of Anadyr II, the famous lead dog of Earl and Natalie Norris (owners of the Alaskan Anadyr kennels in Alaska).

Probably Goosack's star offspring was Ch. Zoox Gadzheek, who performed with great credit on the trail for Ian McRae, and, when shown by Christine McRae, achieved noteworthy success in the show ring including Best of Breed at Crufts in 1986. This was the first year that Challenge Certificates had been awarded to the breed, and Crufts offered the first set. At the time that Champion status was first offered to the breed, there was some controversy as to whether or not the breed was ready to step into the limelight. However, the status was awarded and the popularity of the breed continued to increase.

Goosack features in the pedigrees of many of Britain's top working and show Siberians. Ch. Forstal Meshka, a grandson of Goosack, excelled in lead for Ali Koops for many years, winning thirteen Challenge Certificates including Crufts BOB and then Reserve in the Working Group at Crufts, and becoming the first Siberian to win Best in Show at a General Championship show in Scotland in 1990. A grey and white, he sired three other Champions, Ch. Zima Zareenah of Wapello, owned by Sean and Janice Martin and bred by Simon and Sheila Luxmoore, Ch. Alasam's Cold as Christmas (ex Skimarque Grey Dawn), a grey and white owned by Mary Davidson, and Ch. Forstal Nikolaas, a grey and white originally owned and bred by Liz Leich, whose Forstal kennel prefix was passed on to Sally and Sheril Leich, Ali Koops and Brian Skilton.

CHAMPIONS IN THE RING AND ON THE TRAIL

Ch. Zima Zareenah's dam was Ch. Zima Zala Snyegoorachka, owned and bred by the Luxmoores. Beany, as she was known, won Best Opposite Sex at Crufts in 1986, the first bitch Challenge Certificate on offer in the UK. She won BOB at Crufts the following year and Best In Show at the inaugural Siberian Husky Club of Great Britain Championship show, judged by Nancy Van Gelderen-Parker. A grey and white, she ran on many race-winning teams for

Goosack of Kolyma features in many Siberian pedigrees.

Ch. Zima Zala Snyegoorachka, the first to win a bitch Challenge Certificate in the UK.

Roy-a-Lin's Apatchy Girl of Forstal, an influential US piebald import.

the Zima kennel. Beany's sire was Wapahkwa's Avik, a grey and white imported from Canada in 1975 by Nora Taylor, and sire of seven litters. He was the grandsire of Ch. Valchonok's Prince of Forstal, BOB at Crufts in 1988.

Two other notable lead dogs and show Champions sired by Goosack were Ch. Forstal Kooshak and Ch. Forstal's Annyka of Zima. These bitches were both piebald (at one time an unfashionable colour in the USA which did not win top honours in the show ring). Kooshak was the mother of Meshka. Annyka was the mother of another great Champion, Ch. Zima Toaki. Toaki had an exceptional record, having won more Challenge Certificates (33) and more racing Championship titles (5) and runner-up positions (3) on the trail than any other Siberian. At the age of 10 years and 9 months, having led the Zima team to his fourth Championship title on the trail, he won his fourth Crufts Challenge Certificate having been Best of Breed in 1992 and 1995. Toaki, and others, illustrate the true versatility of this breed – literally out on the trail one

day and in the show ring (following a quick bath!) the next.

Roy-a-Lin's Apatchy Girl of Forstal, another piebald bitch, had been a generous gift from Linda Arnett of the USA to the Leich family and arrived in whelp in 1975. As there were so few lines in the UK at the time, she was a welcome addition. The litter promised to make an outstanding contribution to the breed in the country, but tragically glaucoma was identified and the opportunity to develop these lines was lost. Patchy was the mother of Kooshak.

We have mentioned Lyscha, Goosack's companion through quarantine. The two of them were the best working dogs seen in the UK to that date in the early 1980s and arguably would have held their own with the top sled dogs of any age. Lyscha's skill and intelligence as a lead dog were passed to Annyka who, in turn, proved to be the most successful and intelligent of female leaders for the Luxmoores.

In 1983, Anna Sanchez imported, from Canada, Snowmist's Omega, a grey and white bitch from the Ramey family.

Snowmist's Omega of Asturias, a Canadian import from a great working line.

Omega brought with her the excellent working line of Doc Lombard's Igloo Pak kennel and was the dam of Joi Barnes's Ch. Asturias Vatrushka.

In 1984, Christine Jackson returned to England from a spell in Germany bringing with her Dubchek of Mikrischa, a grandson of Ilya of Northwood and a son of Kenstaff Sascha. Ch. Zoox Dukara and Ch. Zoox Miduchenka (winner of 17 Challenge Certificates) were both daughters of Dubchek.

RECENT IMPORTS

Starting in the late 1970s, running Siberians in harness in competition increased in popularity, with a number of people importing proven sled dogs which had achieved success running on teams in the USA or in Europe.

Notable among these was the introduction of Doug Willett's Sepp-Alta Siberians. In the early seventies, Doug undertook to revive the lines of Markovo stock (belonging to J. Bragg of Canada)

which were from the Seppala strain of Siberians – a very distinct line renowned for their mental toughness, their personality and temperament: a delight to work and live with. John and Kari Coyne brought Rachel and Queen of Sepp-Alta to the UK in 1987. Nutuk of Sepp-Alta arrived in 1988, imported by Peter Carroll from Anneliese Braun-Witschel.

Rachel arrived in whelp and had her litter in quarantine. This litter contained several outstanding working dogs. Of these, Chukchi's Ditko of Sepp-Alta won two racing Championships with the Luxmoores, running in lead. The toughness of the line was shown when he continued to perform with great success despite losing an eye in an accident. Shango, Bear, Sunday, Helen and Ruby, his littermates, were all above-average performers. Sadly this was to be Rachel's only litter in the UK, since she contracted an infection and died in quarantine.

Ch. Skiivolk Ivan (pictured opposite) and Ch. Skiivolk Great Travis, both bred by Jenny Littlejohn and both grandchildren of Rachel, became Champions in 1994 and 1995. Ch. Kazachye's Susitna from a Rajarani, who gained her title in 1995, was a granddaughter of Nutuk of Sepp-Alta.

In the late 1980s Garth and Jenny Littlejohn imported Alaskan Anadyr stock from Holland to their Skiivolk kennel. This was followed in 1990 with Alaskan's Nikolai III of Anadyr from Alaska.

Ch. Skiivolk Ivan, bred by Jenny Littlejohn.

In 1990 the Luxmoores imported Alchi's Shannon from Leigh and Susan Gilchrist's Lokiboden kennel in Ontario, Canada. This introduced the Lokiboden/Igloo Pak line to the UK, and was followed by further imports from the Gilchrists by Fred and Lisa Palmer, with Vista's Amanda of Lokiboden, and by John and Lorraine Carter with Lokiboden's Barrow and Lokiboden's Superior.

Britain has limited space for running Huskies. The sport is highly visible and we retain our ability to run dogs by a careful and responsible attitude to the environment and other forest users and by the fact that there is no money to be made from racing. It is this that has made it so important to ensure that the temptation to import Alaskan Huskies and turn our sport into an even more competitive one, with race purses to match, be resisted. The media can understand and appreciate running Huskies but might be inclined to a very different view of running crossbreeds, hounds and any other dog.

OBEDIENCE AND AGILITY
Very few Siberians are working in competitive Obedience in the UK.

Not many are prepared to take on the challenge, and training any dog for competition takes time and total dedication.

However, there are exceptions: Irene Stapley has trained her Siberian, Cheechako's Eugency (Kodii) to a very high standard. Until recently, he worked in class B at Open and Championship Obedience shows, and he was also able to work a good C class. His wins included four firsts in Novice, three firsts in class A and a second in class B. He is now retired.

Irene uses the reward method, along with play when training, and this seems to work well with the Siberian. She believes in the three Ps – patience, perseverance and praise. Irene is a dedicated and top-class trainer, having won Crufts Supreme Obedience Championship with a Border Collie. She now has a new Siberian called Rajarani Simply Red who is coming on extremely well and should shortly be making his Obedience ring debut. There is little doubt that he too will be an excellent competitor!

Another dedicated Obedience enthusiast in the UK is Julie Maguire. All four of her Siberians are trained to beginner/novice standard, including Heel on Lead, Heel Free, Recall, Retrieve, Sit and Down Stays. Julie occasionally takes part in competitive Obedience.

In Agility there are few, if any, Siberians taking part competitively in the UK although some are trained just for fun.

133

With hard work Siberians can do surprisingly well in Obedience. Pictured: Julie Maguire with Rajarani Treshka.

Kathy Kopelles McCleod with Akela's Chilkat (Chilli) tackling an Agility course.

They love it but tend to become overexcited and play the clown if given the chance! One dog bred by Julie Maguire, Akela's Chilkat, who was exported to Australia, works in competitive Agility and has passed his first trial towards his Agility Dog title: he needs to pass two more.

He is quick and accurate when he wants to be, but can also play the joker. He currently has his CD (Companion Dog) title and is trained by Kathy Kopelles McCleod who, again, is very dedicated to her dogs and their training.

There can be no doubt that, because of the Siberian's intelligence, adaptability and trainability, they can be trained to a high level of Obedience.

BREED CLUBS

The Siberian Husky Club of Great Britain (SHCGB) held its inaugural meeting in 1977. There were twenty-five founder members. At first the club tended to confine its activities to providing information on the breed and a welfare service but, in 1978, the first teach-in was held to inform judges of the essential breed characteristics.

The first working rallies were held in 1978 and 1979 – amateur by today's standards but a start nevertheless. The first rally was held at Hankley Common in Surrey with seven teams entered. Of those present most are still actively involved with Siberians today. They were Heather Lyons, Mags Holt, Sally Leich, Sheril Leich, Mike Harrison, Sandra

Bayliss and Trevor Plant. Rigs were 200lbs compared to today's 35lb versions, with dogs pulling through heavy sand and still having a great time! In the early days, for many, the aim was to get off the start line and out of sight before the dogs stopped for a sniff or a look in the hedgerows. Nowadays the profession-alism exhibited by most teams is almost off-putting for the beginner who finds it difficult to imagine how to get their dogs to the same very high standard. However, the racing world is very friendly and help is always at hand to get people started.

Classes for 5/6 and 3/4 dog teams were scheduled in the early years but the introduction of a 2-dog class was instrumental in allowing many more people to take part without having to take on too many dogs for their circumstances. A 3-dog class has been another popular addition to some races, but open class racing (unlimited numbers) is not generally considered best suited to the twists and turns of British forests. For so many people, once 'bitten' by the racing bug, it is almost impossible to get away. The excitement and enjoyment of the dogs is contagious, whether training in the quiet of the forest or taking part in races.

On the show scene, prior to 1972, Siberians had to compete in the Any Variety classification and this continued until the 1980s when shows started to schedule separate classes for Siberians. By 1990, things had changed dramatically

with no less than six shows scheduling classes for Siberians on the same day!

By 1975, there were some 55 Siberians in the country with numbers growing steadily but with no sign of the explosion in popularity to come in the mid-1980s. Records show that, in 1980, 36 Siberians were registered with the Kennel Club. In 1989, the annual registrations were up to 292, and, in 2000, the Kennel Club registered 961 Siberians.

In 1982, three working rallies were scheduled. In early 1983, the first sled dog race in Scotland was organised by the Coynes. The ensuing publicity ensured that this was a watershed for the breed in the UK.

On the show scene, Siberians were exhibited at Crufts under Any Variety from 1974 to 1986, when the first set of Challenge Certificates was awarded. Following this period, the SHCGB had a number of difficult issues to deal with. Firstly, an undeveloped judges' list, both of breed specialists and all-rounders, was faced with the demands of awarding CCs. Given the 27 sets of CCs on offer at Championship shows in the UK today, the judges' list remains extremely limited.

The second problem was that there were too many CCs on offer, given the still relatively few quality adult Siberians in the country and the lack of judges. The third, and what proved to be the most complex problem, was the working aspirations of Siberian owners, who sought to race and compete, increasing the challenge both to themselves and their dogs, on dirt trails in the UK. These aspirations were not satisfied by the breed club's working calendar of the time and resulted in the formation of a separate working organisation.

The SHCGB has always encouraged a firm and proactive attitude towards health screening for inherited diseases. Dogs are regularly checked for eye conditions and breeding stock is X-rayed for hip dysplasia. By carrying out these checks the Club has successfully ensured that Siberians in the UK are fit and healthy and any problems which may crop up are identified and avoided for future generations.

The Scottish Siberian Husky Club, recognised in 1996, has also taken a proactive attitude towards health screening. With its growing membership it will be hoping to schedule Championship shows in the near future.

WORKING ORGANISATIONS

Various national working organisations were formed during the 1990s to progress the working side of the Siberian. Notable among these were the British Sled Dog Racing Association (BSDRA) (1992-1996), the British Siberian Husky Racing Association (BSHRA) (formed in 1996), and the Sled Dog Association of Scotland (SDAS) which was formed in the early 90s. Other smaller societies and conglomerates have worked together to co-ordinate activities, but have not provided the lasting impact of these associations.

The British Sled Dog Racing Association was formed with the objectives of administering a British Championship and providing top-quality competitive races on quality trails, with a good organisational structure. Backed by a generous sponsorship deal from Labatts, the Canadian corporation, this is exactly what happened over a four-year period.

In 1996, the BSDRA founders agreed that there was a need for further development in the sport, and two new organisations were formed.

Today, the SHCGB, the SDAS and BSHRA each provide full race calendars, with the latter two arranging annual national working Championships. The popularity of racing on dirt in the UK cannot be overstated, with well over 50 races scheduled annually. The top teams would provide quality competition for any team of Siberians in any country.

SOME TOP KENNELS

The most successful kennels over the past two decades, both on the trail and in the show ring, have been Forstal (the Leich family) and Zima (the Luxmoores).

When Don and Liz Leich returned from the US bringing a couple of Siberians with them, they can hardly have imagined the long-term effect this would have on their family. Sally, Sheril and, to a lesser extent Jenny, all became involved with the dogs and their breeding, training and racing. The arrival from Holland in 1980 of Ali Koops to the household, introduced another willing participant in

Ch. Zima Toaki – Champion on the trail and in the show ring.

the all-encompassing lifestyle. Brian Skilton who has been highly successful in both the 4- and 6-dog classes – winning both Championships in recent years – joined the household in 1989.

Simon and Sheila Luxmoore began in 1981 with their first Siberian – a black and white bitch from Christine and David Emery – Lanivet's Zolushka of Zima. They were soon 'bitten by the bug' and successful breeding and buying in of dogs over the years have ensured that Simon has remained at the top of the racing and show scenes throughout their time in the breed.

In the 1980s, Zoox (McRae) were successful both on the trail and in the show ring. In the early and mid-1980s, the show ring was dominated by three memorable dogs: Forstal Mikishar the Amarok, Forstal Noushka, owned by Keith MacCallum, and Forstal's Togo of Asturias, owned by Anna Sanchez.

During the 1990s, the successful affixes in the show ring have included Skiivolk

(Jenny Littlejohn), Aceca (Bruce and Lyn Hall), Azgard (Chris Barry), and Rajarani (Brunette Greenland).

Others who have stood the test of time and continue to both show and race their dogs, having first become involved with Siberians in the early 80s, are Brian and Diane Gale (Orlov), Julie Foard (Bifrost), Helen Lightfoot (Footlite), Ray Ball, Sue and Roger Hull (Nunatak) and others. Yet more have come and gone along the way – in some cases they have ceased their interest purely because of limited space for the number of dogs needed to remain competitive; others have lost interest owing to the level of involvement and dedication required.

OVERSEAS ASSISTANCE
Natalie Norris (Anadyr), an Alaskan Hall of Fame member, spoke to the breed and judged a match as far back as 1984. Doug Willett (Sepp-Alta) visited in 1986, work-testing individual dogs and providing a candid assessment. This was followed up by a presentation on the Seppala Siberian bloodlines.

In 1989, Leigh and Susan Gilchrist (Lokiboden) from Ontario, Canada, gave seminars on their work in the area of skeletal measurement and its relationship to world-class performance in sled dogs. There have been others who have visited and provided input.

When these notable individuals visited the UK in the early years, providing immense knowledge, help and insight to the breed, it can be said in retrospect that more might have been gained from their visits. Each of us is at a different stage in our learning process at any point in time so, for some, these individuals were perhaps too expert at the time; however, most took something of benefit from them. It would be too simplistic to suggest therefore that compulsory attendance might have helped us with today's diversity in type!

Educational inputs like these are critical to the continuing development of the breed in Great Britain. In recent years people have travelled more widely to visit and study Siberian kennels abroad. In addition, newcomers to the breed have the opportunity to visit a number of folk in the UK with established kennels who have been involved in the breed for many years, and can provide a benchmark.

Ch. Forstal Meshka – an outstanding show and working dog. Courtesy: David Dalton.

Recently the importation of Siberians to the UK has grown, particularly of what might be described as overseas show stock. The UK has always prided itself on maintaining the working Siberian Husky. Every effort has been, and will continue to be, made to retain the Siberian Husky in the 'form follows function' standard which is so important to retain the credibility of the breed.

The damaging splits which have occurred in almost every other country, where the working Siberian has become a separate entity from the Siberian that is shown, must be avoided at all costs if we wish to retain a single Siberian Husky breed in the UK. It has always been possible to import 'show type' Siberians, and those who have done so in recent years might well ask why those of us already in the breed did not do so years ago. It was certainly not because we were unable to do so. We chose not to in order to retain the breed we love as the superb athletes they truly are. It has taken a great deal of perseverance and hard work for those who both show and work their Siberians to maintain a dog which performs with great credibility in both areas. While we currently have a wide diversity of type in the UK, this is a healthy position providing that diversity does not split into two 'distinct' types.

Incorporating different lines ensures that the breed remains healthy, fit and able to do the job for which it was originally bred while remaining a handsome and attractive breed.

10 *SIBERIANS IN NORTH AMERICA*

CANADA

Canada's first Siberian Huskie (the original Canadian spelling until the mid-1960s) was registered in October 1939, nine years after the first registration in the US. A total of 38 Siberians were registered at that time by Harry Wheeler from St Jovite in Quebec, who was then the sole breeder in Canada.

HARRY WHEELER

Harry began breeding in 1930 in co-operation with Leonard Seppala and Mrs Elizabeth Ricker. He started with two imports from Siberia named Kingeak and Pearl, three dogs from Seppala, and four or five dogs from Mrs Ricker. These original Siberians were obtained through the Seppala Kennels of Ricker and Seppala in Poland Springs, Maine.

During the war years little breeding took place. There were several litters in 1945, 1946 and 1947, but then Harry stopped breeding and in 1950 he sold everything – the dogs, his kennel name (Seppala), and all his equipment to C.S. Maclean and J.D. McFaul. These two people owned the Gatineau Kennel and bred this stock from 1942 to 1951. This kennel was the second major kennel of Siberians in Canada and a very important one in the history of the breed.

The foundation dogs of the Gatineau strain were Foxstand's Saint, a male, Foxstand's Skivar II, also a male, and Bayou of Foxstand, a bitch. McFaul acquired them from William Shearer, who was an early New England breeder and Champion sled dog racer. The Gatineau strain produced a number of white Siberians including the most famous representatives Nicko, Starina, Timmie, Czarina, Kosko and Tina. Almost all white Siberians today are descended from Gatineau dogs.

When Don McFaul acquired the Wheeler Kennels he ceased to breed his Gatineau stock and made little use of it in his Seppala line. Though no original stock survives now, several excellent racing bloodlines in Canada and the USA owe their high quality to a Gatineau foundation, for example White Water Lake, Bow Lake and Little Alaska.

Tony Landry of White Water Lake Kennels, Ontario, started with two Gatineau males, Kobe of Gatineau and Kosko of Gatineau, plus a bitch named Queen of Gatineau II. He bred Siberians from 1947 to 1966 and one of his dogs, Spook of White Water Lake, can still be found in pedigrees today.

Only once did Don McFaul use a Gatineau dog to sire Seppala stock. That was in 1953. In addition to this, he obtained two more Foxstand dogs: Foxstand's Sunday, a male, and Foxstand's Georgia, a bitch, both of which were used extensively in the Seppala line. Sunday was an excellent, intelligent leader and became a very popular stud of the 1950s.

Austin Moorcroft from Ontario, who owned Huskie Haven Kennels, had a small foundation of stock but had a significant influence on the breed in Canada. His stud was Charney of Seppala, and he had a bitch, Dina of Seppala, and Nony of White, another bitch from Tony Landry's White Water Lake Kennel. He later traded two of his puppies, Yaddam and Ava of Huskie Haven, for two Anadyr dogs, Painuk of Anadyr and Akiak of Anadyr. Yaddam and Ava became part of Earl and Natalie Norris's foundation for their Anadyr

Kennel, which is still going strong today. Many Huskie Haven puppies were shipped all over North America despite the inaccessible location of the kennels in Northern Ontario.

Ch. Ilya of Huskie Haven, a silver grey and white female, became the first Canadian Champion in Toronto in 1951.

Ch. Snow Ridge Chiefson was the first Siberian in Canada to win a Best in Show award. Bunty Dunlop, the daughter of Elizabeth Ricker Nansen, bred this black and white male. The Snow Ridge Kennel was active from 1950 to 1970, producing several Champions including Ch. Snow Ridge Jetson, Ch. Snow Ridge Nanook, Ch. Snow Ridge Oolik and Ch. Katrina of Snow Ridge, mostly in the late 1950s.

Also at this time Bunty acquired several Seppala (McFaul) dogs. Among them were Lobo of Seppala, Laki of Seppala and Ditko of Seppala. Ditko of Seppala can be found in many Sepp-Alta pedigrees today (the kennel name of Doug Willett). Another acquisition at the same time was Bryar's Texas, a leader from Keith and Jean Bryar's kennels in New Hampshire. This dog was shown to his Championship and led the Snow Ridge racing team for a number of years.

During the 1950s, the Seppala name was synonymous with the finest racing Siberians obtainable and such names as Wabask of Seppala, Boyarka of Seppala (Beaver), and Wesen of Seppala (Wes), are still remembered by Champion racers in Alaska and New England.

Two fine racing bloodlines founded on

Dushka of Seppala was instrumental in the formation of the Markovo kennel.

Seppala stock during this period were the Bryar kennels in New Hampshire and the Malamak kennels of J.M. McDougall in Quebec. Well-known Seppala dams are Nina, Zaza, and Mitzie. Mitzie, McFaul's best producing female, also raced until the age of 12 years!

In the fall of 1963, McFaul sold the last of his stock to Earl Norris of the Alaskan Anadyr Kennels in Willow, Alaska. Shango of Seppala, Ditko of Seppala, (both males) and Dushka of Seppala, were the foundation stock of the Markovo kennels of J. Jeffrey Bragg.

Mrs Eva Havlicek of Shady Lane Kennel in Jerseyville, Ontario, was active from 1955 to 1967. Her foundation stock was from Gatineau lines, plus one Sakonnet male from Mrs Elizabeth Nansen (formerly Ricker). Mrs Havlicek showed several dogs of her own breeding to their Championships, including the male Ch. Shady Lane's Nicklas and the bitch Ch. Shady Lane's Tawnsy. Ch. Shady Lane's Kolyma Princess CD was the first Siberian to receive an Obedience title in Canada (Igloo Pak's Suggen ex Katcha of Gatineau).

The Malamak kennels were active from 1959 to 1972 and started with dogs from Gagnon and McFaul Seppalas. The best known of these were the bitches Gagnon's Ruby, Ch. Vixen of Seppala IV and Ch. Chugach of Seppala, and the males Maquois of Seppala and Ch. Sargo of Seppala II. Although renowned as a top racing kennel, Malamak also showed several Seppala foundation animals to their Championships. Many of this stock also became foundation breeding stock in kennels in Quebec and Ontario.

Ch. Racecrest's Bandit (Ch. Snow Ridge Chiefson ex Ch. Shady Lane's Kolyma Princess CD), a long-coat, came from a primarily show kennel; he was one of the most widely used studs in Ontario during the 1960s.

REVIVING THE SEPPALA LINE
Jeff and Mary Bragg from Pefferlaw, Ontario began their Tadluk Kennels in 1968. Their first Siberian was Ch. Racecrest's Openwood Thunder followed by Ch. Troika's Boika. Later they imported a number of Siberians from the Anadyr Kennel in Alaska including two males, Sepp of Anadyr and Fox of Anadyr, and the bitch Laska of Anadyr. Several dogs were also brought in from the eastern USA – Tonto of Calivali, Star of Calivali, Cheenah's Thrush and Ne-

Tuk's Vulcan of Manahtok; the latter two being of Little Alaska lineage.

Tadluk endeavoured to produce type, sound conformation and working ability and bred mainly from established racing lines. Some outside studs included Alakasan's Zhoolik O'Racecrest, Warlock's Hector of Kadatuk, Igloo Pak's Jan, Malamak's Okleasik, Yeso Pac's Red Sleeves and Saber of Calivali. Some of their best-known show dogs were Ch. Troika's Boika, Ch. Tadluk's Edmonton and Ch. Tadluk's Flidget.

Tadluk dogs were sold across Canada and the US for both showing and racing purposes and will be found behind a number of present-day kennels.

When Jeff decided to concentrate on the Seppala line of Siberians, Mary continued breeding under the Tadluk name until 1975, when the kennel was dispersed. Jeff (who later moved to Saskatchewan), continued breeding from his Markovo kennel from 1968 to 1975. His foundation male stock were Shango and Ditko of Seppala, and Ch. Mikiuk Tuktu of Tornyale. Dushka of Seppala, Lyl of Sepsequel and Frostfive of Anisette wove the female foundation for his Markovo Kennel.

Jeff's fondest wish was to restore the Seppala strain and time was of the essence, because the remaining stock of Seppala Siberians was ageing and was scattered across the country. Life was far from easy in Saskatchewan and in 1975 Jeff realised, with the birth of his tenth litter, that this ambitious breeding programme was no longer possible, emotionally or economically. Jeff endeavoured to find buyers for the 11 puppies and 24 adults of pure Seppala lineage. He discovered that there was great interest in the strain he had spent five years to rescue from virtual extinction.

To quote Jeff: "It is now possible for me to believe that they do represent a true and viable alternative to the over-bred show strains and that, through them, there is at least some chance of reshaping the Siberian Husky a bit nearer to the original. My own salvage operation had come to a natural close and I have left the arena of active breeding knowing that there is a sizeable body of sound young stock with which those who are interested and able may carry on the strain. I have every confidence that in their hands it will prosper and develop in soundness and working ability to a far greater extent than it would have on my own."

Twenty years later, Jeff Bragg has returned to breeding, with a kennel in Whitehorse, Yukon, and about 60 dogs. Many of his Seppala stock can be found throughout the US and Europe.

UELEN
Maisie Morrow from Parksville, British Columbia, first established in 1969 but after their first litter Bruce Morrow became interested in the Seppala line and, in a very short time, they procured six Siberians from Jeff

Chiwooka's Illanzer won the best Sled Dog title at the same show as his grandfather (Surgut of Markovo – left) won the best Veteran at the ripe old age of 13 years and 9 months.

Bragg's Markovo kennels. These dogs were Helen of Markovo, Surgut of Markovo, Davik of Markovo, Mokka of Markovo, Sly of Markovo and Zaza of Markovo. Surgut became foundation stock for Bruce's Uelen kennels.

At the age of 13, Surgut won Best Veteran at the Siberian Husky Club of British Columbia in October 1987. Judge Lee Hills wrote that, on seeing him, "visions of the Standard dance through my head". Surgut can be found in many pedigrees behind Sepp-Alta breedings. Chiwooka's Illanzer, a grandson of Surgut owned by Paul and Barbara Fisk, was Best Sled Dog at the same show.

Peter and Judy French started their Sergii kennel in 1972 but, individually, they had been breeding, racing and showing Huskies since 1968. They were instrumental in setting up The Siberian Husky Club of Canada in 1968, so people could share information and knowledge about the breed. Sergii's

best all-round Siberian was Ch. Gustov Happovitch who was also very competitive on the race trail.

SNOWMIST
Beryl, Kim and Sue Ramey established the Snowmist kennel in the spring of 1973. In the beginning, they showed and raced all the dogs they owned, but soon realised that some major changes were needed. In 1978, when Kim met her husband Tom, the Snowmist kennel had started to split into specialised dogs for racing and showing.

Many of Kim and Tom's racing Siberians were evaluated at Sepp (Siberian Evaluation Performance Programme). This programme was designed by a group of concerned Siberian owners because they felt that, due to the continuing popularity of the breed, the Siberian was losing its natural ability to be a fast, tough racing sled dog. Many being bred had never seen a harness and there were fewer and fewer

Siberians appearing in world-class competitive teams. Fearing that the traits essential to a working dog were being lost, a testing programme to identify the Siberians who could still perform at the top level was developed – the idea being that, once tested, the best dogs could be the foundation of future breedings to put the Siberian back on the trail as a respected working/racing dog.

Many of Kim and Tom's foundation stock came from the Anadyr Kennel and, later on, they introduced some Igloo Pak, Lokiboden and Zero bloodlines as outcrosses to try to improve their performance. Alaskan's Larka of Anadyr was one of their best-ever sled dogs.

Northstar's Snowmist Birch SDU CD won the Ward Young Trophy in 1995 and 1996. This award is given to the dog that qualifies in all three disciplines of Racing, Showing and Obedience within the Siberian Husky Club of Canada's calendar year.

Beryl, Kim and sister Sue showed their other successful dogs to many wins at specialist Canadian shows. Most notable was Can. Am. Ch. Snowmist's Mai Tai and they had an Obedience title

Northstar's Snowmist Birch SDU, CD.
Courtesy: Alex Smith photography.

with Bain's Northern Snocub CD.

Kim says: "Nothing beats the thrill of driving a great team of Siberians over a beautiful trail or showing a home-bred dog to Best in Show!"

TOWMAN
Towman Kennels came into being when Tom and Annette Iliffe bought their first Siberian in 1971 from Tom's father, Ted, who had owned Noweta Siberians for many years. Annette showed Noweta's Lobo to his Championship. Tom and Annette preferred to race their Siberians.

Snowmist team, 1998. Leaders: Lokiboden's Gremlin SD (driver's right, dark face); Snowmist's Keys SDX (driver's left).

Noweta's Lobo. Courtesy: Dal Hubbert.

On one occasion they drove the 3,000 or so miles to Alaska, to bring back Alaskan's Chevak of Anadyr, a female who they bred to Rix's Stormy Buckhorn, a dog Tom greatly admired. The effort proved worthwhile as they started to produce dogs that were achieving results on the race trail. Towman's Yakutat returned to the Norrises and Earl said he was the best outcross he had ever taken back into his kennel.

LOKIBODEN
Leigh and Susan Gilchrist started in 1975 with two pet Huskies and, after seeing their first race, got hooked on the sport and, inevitably, started looking for a property so that they could have more dogs. Their first litter, along with the parents, made up their first racing team in the days of the five-dog class. Fortunately, they started with dogs that had racing lineage and some athletic ability and were successful on the local circuit competing against all types of sled dogs.

The most successful Lokiboden racing dogs have been produced from Igloo Pak lineage. Louise and Doc Lombard (Igloo Pak kennels) provided a wealth of information and were influential in the Gilchrists' breeding and training programmes.

Leigh and Susan purchased Arctic Trail's Kola, an Igloo Pak line bitch, from Lloyd Slocumb and bred her to Igloo Pak's Kaltag to produce their 'Dance' litter, producing Lokiboden's Tango, Twist and Hustle. They later obtained Igloo Pak's Sitka from Doc Lombard and bred her to Tango. Mr Snuffalupagus,

Igloo Pak's Sitka bred by Doc and Louise Lombard, owned by Leigh and Susan Gilchrist.

145

known as Snuffy, came from this 'Sesame Street' litter. Charlie Belford suggested this tight Igloo Pak breeding after watching the dogs run at one of the SEPP evaluations. Many of their best dogs can be traced back to Snuffy and Sitka.

The goal of Lokiboden kennels has been to race with world-class teams and to finish within ten per cent of the leaders. Leigh and Susan strive to attain their goal by producing dogs that have smooth, effortless gaits, a good work ethic, endurance and friendly temperaments. Leigh developed a skeletal structural norm for racing sled dogs based on measurements taken by Susan of dogs on top unlimited class racing teams. This has also had some influence on their breeding programme.

The Gilchrists were involved in setting up the SEPP project and they now

measure participating dogs. Their kennel has grown from five dogs in the 70s to about 30 dogs. They believe that this is a minimum number if they are to produce quality racing Siberian Huskies. One of their favourite mottoes is "Performance is a priority, not an option".

KIMLAN

Kimlan Kennel was also registered in 1975. Don and Rosemary Hooker spent a lot of time visiting several kennels but kept going back to Charlie and Carolyn Posey's Yeso Pac Kennel to see their beautiful dual purpose dogs. A couple of years later they acquired Yeso Pac's Grey Wolf when the Poseys stopped running their team. They thought he would help their fledgling team – this he did and far more. Watching Grey Wolf's exceptional movement as he raced around their yard, they decided to show him. They not only made him a Canadian Champion but an American Champion too, at the age of nine. He became the main stud dog in their kennel and virtually every dog they own descends from him.

OTHER KENNELS

Ch. Pikwutuske's Grey Phantom CD, known as Duppy, is the reason why Brent and Kathy Thomas moved out from town to country to work and support their dogs. Duppy and Ch. Yeti's Kola (a red and white) are behind Ch. Telaka's Kamper. Ch. Xango Zirka Telaka Yeti, together with Kamper, achieved a Best Brace in Show in Winnipeg.

Leigh Gilchrist's Lokiboden team, 1990.

Ch. Kanunik's White Knight, one of the kennel's two piebald Champions.

Sandy Cairns acquired Azura, OTCh. Trailmasters Soomi, her first Siberian Husky, in 1971 and she was an Obedience winner in 1979, being the first Siberian to be placed in the Working Group in Obedience. Azura was quite a character and trained Sandy well! Ch. Shisando's Frostkist Footman, known as Eli, was from Sandy Cairns' first litter and became her first home-bred Champion. He won many awards and at the age of 10 he won the Companion Dog (CD) title.

Kathy Stewart's Kanunik Kennels have had Siberians for more than 21 years and have succeeded in producing and owning many Champions. They originally started with a dog from Monadnock lines. Ch. Baron Nicholas Von Gower was their first Champion and Obedience dog and also their foundation stud for Kanunik kennels. Over the years they also made up two piebald Champions, Ch. Kanunik's Kreme Puff and Ch. Kanunik's White Knight.

Richard Smith, a Royal Canadian Mounted Policeman (RCMP), who became involved with Siberians in the late 70s, used his team instead of a snow bike on official RCMP back country patrols in the rugged terrain of the Northwest Territories. He later used his team for guided tours and in 1980 he undertook to retrace the historic North West Mounted Police and Hudson Bay Company dog sled patrol routes from Fort Edmonton, Alberta to Old Crow, Yukon, a 2,600-km journey.

RACING IN CANADA
There are many races in Canada but ranking among the important historical derbies were the St. Agathe, the Maniwaki and the Quebec City, all in Quebec, and also The Pas, Manitoba. Today, The Pas is the only one still in existence. It is special because it is a mass start race on a lake that funnels down to one trail on a river. It is a three-day event and is known to be challenging.

Among the best known of the North American races still held today are the Yukon Quest, The Labrador 400, The Iditarod Trail and the Fur Rondy. Many of these races cross the borders of Alaska, Canada and the Northern United States.

THE UNITED STATES
by Pam Thomas
Siberians have been in North America since 1908 and in the 'lower' 48 states (the original 48 United States excluding Alaska and Hawaii) since 1926, when Leonard Seppala, accompanied by 42

Ch. Wonalancet's Baldy of Alyeska.

dogs, went on tour after the Serum Run (see the History chapter). It is safe to say that virtually all Siberians in the United States descend from a handful of those dogs, or dogs subsequently imported to the continental US in the 1930s. In many cases the Siberian owner can trace his or her dog's pedigree back to the 'original' imports to Nome, Alaska by Seppala; to dogs such as Dolly, Kayak and Rauna.

THE ORIGINAL DOGS

Unfortunately, photographs of many of the dog teams and of individual dogs of the day are not identified and so we may, in fact, have pictures of Molinka, for instance – we just do not know it because she is not named. We do have an identified photograph of Dolly. Evidence points to Dolly being one of the original imports from the Kolyma River area, but it is not known when or by whom. She is not seen in photographs of Seppala's 1915 All Alaska Sweepstake team.

Dolly was bred to Sepp and produced Fritz, and to Suggen to produce Togo. Fritz was born in 1915 and was owned by the Pioneer Mining Company. He is seen in photographs of Seppala's 1916 Sweep-stakes team and in lead in photographs of Victor Anderson's 2nd place All Alaska Sweepstakes team in 1917. Seppala was given ownership of the dogs in 1924. Fritz ran on the 1925 Serum Run team and went to New England with Seppala in 1926. He is then seen running lead for Elizabeth Ricker in 1927 and for Dr Francis J.

D'Avignon in 1929. Records show he was sold to Dr Beverley Sproul and died in December 1932 in New York.

Fritz was bred to Shika (Ugruk ex Boorka) to produce Harry, who was bred to Kolyma (Putza ex Duska) to produce Toska, Bonzo, Chernook (or Chenuk), and Rosie in 1925. Tosca was bred in New England to Smoky to produce Belford's Wolf. She went to Harry Wheeler's kennel in Quebec and produced five litters out of the 1930s import Kreevanka. Ch. Vanka of Seppala II (Cossack) was born to Kreevanka and Tosca in 1935. In 1942, Cossack was bred to Sky of Seppala (Smokey of Seppala ex Nanna) to produce Ch. Helen of Cold River and Duchess of Cold River. Mrs Marie Lee Frothingham owned Sky.

AFTER WORLD WAR II

William Belletete eventually obtained Duchess from William Shearer, who had obtained ownership of several dogs from the Army at the end of World War II – from the Arctic Search and Rescue Unit

Alaskan's Yakut of Anadyr II, one of the finest American Siberians.

and the Dog Ambulance Corps. Duchess was subsequently bred to Eva (Short) and Milton Seeley's Ch. Wonalancet's Baldy of Alyeska in 1948 and produced two males who had a profound influence on the breed. Kiev of Gap Mountain was used to illustrate the Breed Standard for many years and Izok of Gap Mountain became one of the most influential studs, and was described as an enthusiastic, hard-driving, steady sled dog. There was another brother, Baldy of Gap Mountain, who was bred at least once, but very little is written about this dog.

Izok was bred to any number of bitches: to Ch. Aleka's Czarina to produce Mulpus Brook's The Roadmaster; to Panda Girl, producing Monadnock's Kira and Monadnock's Laska; to Tanya of Monadnock to produce Monadnock's Petya; to Aleka's Sonya, producing Sonya's Torger; to Monadnock's Czarina to produce Monadnock's Aleka; to Rola to produce Wanee of Marly (the foundation bitch for Marlytuk) and Ch. Noonok of Marly. These offspring, or their siblings, appear in most racing and showing pedigrees in North America today, including Peggy Koehler's Alakazan bloodlines. Izok is, to this day, held in high regard by Peggy and, according to *The Complete Siberian Husky* by Demidoff and Jennings, was the focus of the breeding programme of Jack and Donna Foster's Frosty Aire Kennel. After seeing him, they "aimed at producing dogs of the type and calibre of famous Izok of Gap Mountain".

BEAUTIES OF THE BREED

Alaskan's Yakut of Anadyr II (Towman's Yakutat ex Yeso Pac's Joni of Anadyr) is a lovely example of the breed. Bred and owned by Earl and Natalie Norris, Yakut has run the Iditarod Trail Sled Dog race three times in lead, the HOPE race across the Kamchatka Peninsula once (coming 3rd), and numerous other distance races. She has been shown only rarely, winning an Award of Merit at the 1995 Siberian Husky Club of Anchorage Specialty in 1996. Yakut is used as the 'standard' dog for judges' education seminars, as she is very close to perfect proportionally. She also won the Sled Bitch class and Best Sled Dog at the 1998 National Specialty.

Incidentally, the first HOPE race was organised in 1991 by Jon Van Zyle, Leo Rasmussen and a couple of other people. It was a sled dog journey between Nome, Alaska and Anadyr in Siberia, a distance of 1,200 miles, designed to bring Chukchi drivers and Americans peace,

149

Ch. Alkas'iber's Editorial Comment SDX (Oprah) is renowned for her stride.

co-operation and, above all, hope for a better and friendlier world and, wrote Jon Van Zyle, "all of this was accomplished under the guise of man's best friend".

Izok of Gap Mountain represents the seventh generation in Yakut's pedigree on her sire's side. In this case, Izok was bred to Aleka's Sonya (by Jean Bryar) to produce Tamara, the dam of Bryar's Texas. Texas was the sire of Ch. Wobiska's Chippy of Roka, who was the dam of Kelson's Elko, a Canadian dog and an influential male in current racing lines in both the US and Canada. Elko and/or his female siblings, Kelson's Goblin and Kelson's Ginger, are found in the bloodlines of Lokiboden, Anadyr, Alkas'iber, Wolfepak, Snowmist, Sepp-Alta, Kodiak, and others. In Yakut's pedigree, Elko produced Rix's Stormy O'Buckhorn, who, in turn, produced Yakut's sire, Towman's Yakutat.

Ch. Alkas'iber's Editorial Comment,

SDX (Alkas'iber's Steely Dan, SDX ex Keewatin's Mighty Mishka, SDO), known as Oprah and bred by George and Ann Cook, was born in 1989, and ran the Yukon Quest in 1992 as a young leader. She and her mother, leader of the 1989 Lombard/Norris Award team, ran Marmora, Labrador, the Can-Am, and other distance races. Oprah finished her Championship in December 1996. Her owners gave her greatest strength as a ground-covering, effortless stride.

Oprah's pedigree shows Izok of Gap Mountain to be eight generations back, but follows the same path through Tamara, Bryar's Texas and Ch. Wobiska's Chippy of Roka to Kelson's Elko. At this point, Elko was bred to Nekanesu's Sitka (Malamak's Ego ex Ch. Wobiska Tasha of Nekanesu) to produce Nekanesu's Deno, sire of Nekanesu's Sonny Boy. Sonny produced Oprah's dam, Keewatin's Mighty Mishka SDO (Minnie), a great leader for George and Ann Cook and the first bitch to earn the Sled Dog Outstanding title in the US. Minnie's dam, leader Nekanesu's Lucky, can trace her ancestors back to Bryar's.

Oprah comes from a long line of leaders, and she was most often used to bring the team into a checkpoint reliably. Ann recalls the night Oprah led the team roaring into Dawson under a huge moon. It was so cold, the dogs' breath froze in mid-air and rained crystals on to their heads and backs, giving them all a silver halo that George called Oprah By Moonlight. Oprah's sire, Alkas'iber's

Ch. Alkas'iber's Pumpkin Seed SD, a Show Champion and a veteran of the Yukon Quest.

Ch. Stormwatch's Montana, an accomplished racer and show dog. Courtesy: Bishop Photography.

Steely Dan, SDX was the Cooks' best leader, and his sire, Canadian Champion Channikko's Nordic Digger, Am CD, Can CDX, Can TD, TT. Digger, as he was known, was a fabulous leader, a happy working dog, and a genius with a sense of humour, who is credited with saving the life of a missing three-year-old boy. Digger also logged thousands of hours as a Therapy Dog.

Monte, who is Ch. Stormwatch's Montana (Ch. Black Oaks Arctic Trace ex Black Oak's Arctic Baircrest), has run the Iditarod Trail Sled Dog Race twice, the Yukon Quest once, and numerous other distance races. He took an award of Merit at the 1995 National Specialty from the Sled Dog class, took Best Opposite Sex from the Bred By Exhibitor class at the 1996 Siberian Husky Club of Anchorage Specialty and won Best Opposite Sex at the 1998 Siberian Husky Club of America National Specialty over some 180 other fine bitches and dogs.

Izok of Gap Mountain shows up in Monte's maternal pedigree twelve generations back, behind Ch. Frosty Aire's Banner Boy, CD. Banner was bred to Kameo of Kazan to produce Ch. Alakazan's Nikolai, the sire of Ch. Innisfree's Pegasus, who in turn sired Ch. Innisfree's Lady Shandilar, who is dam of Ch. Black Oak's Winter Stormwatch, CD, SD. Winter sired Black Oak's Arctic Baircrest, the dam of Monte.

Ch. Alkas'iber's Pumpkin Seed, SD (Ch. Dama's Matanuska of Shonko ex Konik's Kountry Pumpkin) was a rookie for the 1992 Yukon Quest team of breeders, Janet and Gary Cingel and George and Ann Cook. Essie, as she is known, is red and was referred to by the veterans at the Quest as "that little golden dog". She has since run Labrador, the Can-Am, and other distance races. She finished her Championship rather quickly in October 1994 on the strength of her floating gait.

Essie's sire, Mat, was a nationally ranked show dog who ran wheel on the Cooks' team. On both sides of Essie's pedigree we find Izok of Gap Mountain ten generations back, behind Ch. Frosty Aire's Banner Boy, CD. Izok was bred to Aleka's Sonya to produce Sonya's Torger. The Fosters then bred Ch. Kenai Kittee of Beauchien CDX, to Sonya's Torger, to produce Frosty Aire's Tobuk, the sire of Ch. Frosty Aire's Beauchien CD, who was the sire of the famous all-Champion litter (five) that included Ch. Frosty Aire's Beau-Tuk Balto. Balto sired Ch. Frosty Aire's Banner Boy.

It is at this point, at Banner Boy, that Essie's pedigree diverges. On her dam's side, Banner Boy produced Ch. Troika's Demishka, who sired Digger. Digger is the sire of Dan, who sired Konik's Kountry Pumpkin, a leader for Gary and Janet Cingel. On Essie's sire's side, Banner Boy produced Ch. Alakazan's Nikolai, sire of Ch. Tawny Hill's Gaibryel who sired Shonko's Dontcha Dare, the sire of Mat. Interestingly, on Essie's dam's side, behind Konik's Silver Streak, is Nicko II of Little Alaska (Leonard of Penn Forest ex Dagwong of Little Alaska) – a double Starina of Gatineau descendent.

MAKING THE CONNECTION

Let us go back to those five litters produced by Kreevanka and Tosca in the early to mid 1930s. We have established that Ch. Vanka of Seppala II figures prominently in today's pedigrees. Burka of Seppala was another of the influential offspring. In 1942, Burka was bred to Delzeue of Cold River (Sapsuk of Seppala ex Chuchi of Seppala) and produced Valuiki of Cold River (foundation dog for Monadnock) and Bugs. Bugs, also known as Cub, was bred to Foxstand's Sukey (born 1940) and produced Candia, a key dog in the Norrises' Alaskan/Anadyr breeding.

T-Cheeakio of Alyeska (born 1938, Belford's Wolf ex Cheeak of Alyeska) was bred to Ipuk of Alyeska (born 1941, Ch. Wonalancet's Baldy of Alyeska ex Cheeak of Alyeska) to produce Keo of Alyeska. She was also bred to Czar of Alyeska (born 1941, Wolfe of Seppala ex Ch. Cheenah of Alyeska) in 1944 to produce Chinook's Alladin of Alyeska. T-Cheeakio was then bred to Ch. Wonalancet's Baldy of Alyeska to produce Alyeska's Kobuk of Chinook in 1949.

Alladin never missed a race in the Norris team from 1947 to 1953 and always ran single lead. He produced

T-Cheeakio of Alyeska from Chinook's kennels.

Natalie and Earl with Alladin, described as "a once-in-a-lifetime dog."

leaders for winning teams such as Kit MacInnes's Women's Alaskan and Women's North American Championship wins led by Oslo. He had a five point major to his name, too.

He was bred, at the Norrises, to Bayou of Foxstand to produce Ch. U-Chee of Anadyr, who figures prominently in Norbert and Kathleen Kanzler's and Charlotte Reynolds's Arctic Kennels behind El Ferro, and Bob and Dorothy Page's Chotovotka kennels behind the Frosty Aire dogs. Bred to Papka of Ananen, Alladin produced Alaskan's Sestra of Anadyr, Alaskan's Tawny Lad of Anadyr, and Alaskan's Chorni of Anadyr. Alladin was bred back to his daughter, Dirka of Anadyr (Alladin ex Candia) to produce Akiak of Anadyr, the dam of Monadnock's Nadya. He was also bred back to his daughter, Ch. U-Chee of Anadyr, to produce Czar of Anadyr, the sire of Ch. Stony River's Ootah (same

litter as Czar of Anadyr and Pasco of Anadyr). These two dogs are behind Ch. Monadnock's Norina, the dam of Ch. Monadnock's Aleka, and Ch. Monadnock's King (son of Ch. Monadnock's Pando).

Yaddam of Husky Haven ex Dirka of Anadyr produced Natasha of Anadyr, Ch. Noho of Anadyr, Carka of Anadyr, and Baridia of Anadyr. Alladin bred to Natasha produced the leader Nebesna of Polaris, dam to Ch. Babbet of Lakota.

Another key dog was Igloo Pak's Tok. He was Doc Lombard's favourite, could run with the Alaskans and did so for several years. Born in 1957, Tok was 12 years old when he ran on the winning Anchorage Fur Rondy team in 1970.

Tok's influence on today's Siberians cannot be underestimated. His offspring can be found behind such dogs as Alaskan's Jafet of Anadyr, Posey's Willewah and Ch. Yeso Pac's Reynard (Yeso Pac and Marlytuk), Ch. Doonauk's Keemah (Doonauk, Marlytuk, Savdajaure), Yeso Pac's Anyia (Yeso Pac, Sno Fame), and any number of primarily racing kennels such as Arctic Trail, Foxhaunt, Little Alaska, Lokiboden, Heritage North, Komet, Natomah, Caribou, Northome, Sepp-Alta and Zero.

OTHER INFLUENTIAL DOGS
Natalie Jubin (Norris) took Chinook's Alladin of Alyeska and ten other dogs with her to Alaska. Candia, acquired from Bill Shearer, was bred to Alladin in 1946 and the Norrises got T-Serko of

Igloo Pak's Tok, still winning races at 12 years of age.

Anadyr and Dirka of Anadyr (dam of Ch. Noho of Anadyr, Carka of Anadyr, Baridia of Anadyr and Natasha of Anadyr). Starina of Gatineau (Foxstand's Saint ex Ilona of Seppala) had been acquired from Don McFaul and was bred, in 1951, to T-Serko of Anadyr to produce Ch. Bonzo of Anadyr CD who, at the age of three, became the first great leader for the Norrises. In 1955 he became the first Siberian to win an all breed Best in Show, and only the fourth Siberian to have both an Obedience title and a Championship. Bonzo's sibling, Tyone of Anadyr, is behind Innisfree's Rashiri of A'Baska and Harding's Gingeroe, who is behind Martha Lake and Kimiluk (Canadian) dogs.

Meanwhile, Short Seeley had bred Alyeska's Kobuk of Chinook to Keo of Alyeska to produce Alyeska's Sugrut of Chinook and Bluie of Chinook in 1953. Sugrut was bred to Monadnock's Flash to produce Columbia's Admiral, sire of Ch. Koonah's Red Kiska. Doc Lombard acquired Sugrut and bred him to Igloo Pak's Misty (Foxstand's Pontiac ex Chogoandoe's Vanya) to produce the famous Igloo Pak's Tok on November 17, 1957. Sometime after that, the Norrises took possession of Sugrut and bred him to Vixen of Anadyr (Carka of Anadyr ex Ava of Husky Haven) to get the fastest dog they have yet owned – Alaskan's Nicolai of Anadyr, born November 10th, 1958 (also in the litter were Alaskan's Polyanka of Anadyr and Alaskan's Vixen of Anadyr II).

Ch. Bonzo of Anadyr CD, was, as Natalie Norris said in *Racing Alaskan Sled Dogs* (Bill Vaudrin, 1976), one of four leaders she and Earl had that "would warrant the label, 'a once-in-a-lifetime dog'. The others were Nicolai (Nicolai II's grandsire), Bonzo, and Alladin. Each was a superior individual in its own right." The above-mentioned book contains articles written by 23 of the greatest names in sled dog racing, such as George Attla, Gareth Wright, Drs Lombard and Belford, Joe Redington Sr and Dick Tozier. It includes biographies of 18 very famous leaders, including Doc Lombard's Nellie, George Attla's Johnny and Blue, Earl and Natalie's Alladin and Bonzo and Kit MacInnes's Ch. Tyndrum's Oslo CDX (Pando of Monadnock x Ch. U-Chee of Anadyr).

Among Bonzo's major accomplishments were keeping Earl and Natalie in the money at Championship races during the mid-1950s, performing beautifully in the Obedience and show rings and in lead dog competitions, and producing a litter with Ch. Babbet of Lakota that would greatly influence breeding programmes far and wide. One of this litter was Alaskan's Bon-Bon of Anadyr, the dam of the famous leader Alaskan's Astro of Anadyr. Two others in this litter, Cawkick of Lakota and Poko Bueno of Lakota, contributed to the breeding programmes at Dichoda and S-K-Mo kennels while the fourth, Alaskan's Babbette of Anadyr, produced four-time Iditarod leader Alaskan's Ko-Ka-Nok of Anadyr, and a fifth, Am. Can. Ch. Chuchi of Anadyr, had great influence on breeding programmes on the west coast of the US and thence Australia, through Huskihaus Indy of Kiska.

THE SPLIT

The first Standard for the Siberian Husky was written in 1930, the year the American Kennel Club recognised the Siberian Husky as a distinct breed. Obviously, this document described dogs such as Fritz, Toto, Togo, Tosca, and Kreevanka, racing dogs all. In fact, the first paragraph of the Standard says: *"He should be exceptionally active, quick and light on his feet, able to run in harness with a load at a speed of twenty miles an hour for short distances."* And, in point of fact, almost all the Siberians bred in the United States at the time did race; breeding decisions were, for the most part, based on the dog's ability to win races for Leonard Seppala, Elizabeth

Bonzo was not only a Champion racer, but also a successful sire, show dog and Obedience competitor.

Ricker, Millie Turner, Harry Wheeler, Bill Shearer, Short Seeley, and others.

It is not a secret that there are now two distinct styles of Siberians in the United States – the 'show' dog and the 'working' dog. This is unfortunate, but probably inevitable in such a large country. Once the breed gained national exposure in the early 1950s several factors conspired to hasten the separation.

Ch. Monadnock's Pando was really famous since, from 1957 to 1961, he had won four Specialty shows and five consecutive Best of Breeds at Westminster; so black and white, blue-eyed Siberians became the prototype of the breed in the public's mind. Short Seeley and Lorna Demidoff were older and did not race any more themselves, but they did show and they based their breeding decisions on winning in the show ring.

The 1950s and 60s were good years for the American economy so people were willing to travel and spend money on dogs. The popularity of the Siberian as a show dog and pet exploded just at the time that the popularity of the Alaskan Husky did as a much faster sled dog. Heat and humidity prevented southern owners from running their dogs, thus breeding decisions were not based on working ability, but rather on producing the head styles and body shapes that would win in the show ring under judges who had no knowledge or experience with the breed.

Seriously-raced Siberians in the US compete against the world's fastest Alaskan Huskies, in both sprint racing and middle- and long-distance races. As "form follows function", Siberians can be competitive against Alaskan Huskies at sprint speeds, travelling at over 19 miles per hour for 6 miles. Distance-trained dogs will tend to travel at an average of 10 to 12 miles per hour for long periods of time.

Dogs that are bred to win in the show ring under the vast majority of approved judges, tend to be shorter dogs, but round-boned and heavier-boned, with a shorter muzzle; they carry more weight, have shorter pasterns, and move with less light-footedness and more rolling of the topline. They tend to have less angulation both front and rear and they rarely, very rarely, have dark faces.

Between the 1950s and the early 1990s, there were few, if any, dogs bred to race competitively that even finished their Championships, much less won well in the show ring. This is not to say that breeders did not try to do both. They found, unfortunately, that those dogs who could become Show Champions were not world-class racing dogs, and vice versa.

PRESENT-DAY DOGS
In the early 1990s, the breed was blessed with several judges who not only understood the Standard, but also were willing to do something out of the ordinary. Granted, there are only a few such judges, but the breed is seeing more top working dogs in the ring now than it has in forty years because of them. Iditarod finishers and middle-distance race winners have won several Specialty shows. Unfortunately, it is doubtful if we will ever see a dog bred to compete in sprint racing finish its Championship. Successful sprint racing dogs are simply too extreme.

11

SIBERIANS WORLDWIDE

AUSTRALIA

In many countries of the world, the history of the Siberian Husky is relatively short. This is certainly true in Australia, where quarantine laws limited the introduction of new breeds to those where one person's enthusiasm overrode the difficulties. In 1971, Derry George became interested in the sled dogs of Antarctica, meeting the ships that came to Melbourne, Victoria, from Australia's Antarctic base in order to load fresh supplies. He learnt a lot about sled dogs from the people he met on these ships. Eventually, after much enquiry in Britain, in 1976 he was able to import a bi-eyed black and white male Siberian from Mrs Leich's Forstal Kennel, called Forstal's Tumac.

In November of the same year came a female, Danlee Karelia, from Mrs Sandra Bayliss of the Danlee Kennels in Britain. Karelia was a silver-grey and white, brown-eyed beauty with a lovely nature. Together, Karelia and Tumac produced the first litter in Australia which was born in September 1978: one male, Myvore Yuri, and two females, Myvore Lara and Michaela.

Myvore Yuri was sold as a family pet and his sister Lara went to John and Carole Perkins from Victoria.

Mitch Blockley team (with Northstar Siberians) winning the Altitude 5000 Pedigree Pal Sled Dog Derby in 1997.

Arrangements were made with Mrs Charlene Wasson (Hunevoss Kennels) of New Zealand for a male to join Lara. Tushin of Hunevoss was imported from New Zealand, his sire (Tameila Rjukaan) and dam (Forstal's Nadia) being the first imports into New Zealand. As Lara came from the first litter born in Australia, so Tushin was from the first litter bred in New Zealand. The Perkins chose the kennel prefix Frostypines and produced a number of litters.

In 1979, Derry George imported another female, Skimarque Duska, from Mrs Jenny Manley's Skimarque Kennels in England. She was red and white with hazel eyes. Skimarque Duska was mated to Forstal's Tumac and in May 1980 she produced the second litter in Australia, which consisted of three males and two females. Derry George kept one female, Myvore Anna, and the males were sold to Mrs Wendy Newton of Victoria (Myvore Ilya) and Mrs Edna Harper of Victoria (Myvore Layka). Layka was the foundation Siberian for Kolyma Kennels. Mrs Lorraine Bell of Western Australia bought Myvore Inuk who became the foundation of Kimoberg Siberians.

Although Myvore Ilya was later sold, Wendy Newton (Chukchi) purchased the first three imports from Derry George. She imported another male from Mrs Lynn Harrison in the UK. Brushbow's Atlatl was a black and white.

Mrs Harper purchased a female, Frostypines Anya, from Carole Perkins, and started her kennel with Myvore Layka and Frostypines Anya. Mrs Harper imported a grey and white, brown-eyed male from Rossfort Kennels, UK – Rossfort Nijinski – and two females from Innisfree Kennels in America: Innisfree N York Touch O' Class, a grey and white with brown eyes, and Innisfree N York Blazing Star, a deep red and white.

Mrs Lorraine Bell also imported a dog – Maicon's Goosak of Kimoberg (red and white bi-eyed), and a bitch, Asturias Zaika (grey/white brown-eyed), Goosak from America, and Zaika from England.

Due to the change in quarantine laws in 1994, which reduced the quarantine period from 180 days to 30 days, many more Siberians are now being imported.

SLED DOGS

The first sled dog event in Australia was held in 1987 in the snow fields of the Victorian Alps. The interest in running Huskies then progressed to the formation of the Siberian Husky Club of Victoria which arranged social sledding events. South Australia was the next state to become involved in running dogs. This led to increased interest in the sport of sled dog racing and, eventually, the first independent club was formed. The Undera Sled Dog Club was formed solely to organise a race every June on the Queen's birthday long weekend. Independent clubs are now operating in Victoria, New South Wales, South Australia and Queensland.

Numerous independent races now make for a busy race season from May to

August (weather and temperature permitting). As most of the snow fields are in National Parks, where dogs are not allowed, there is very limited access to snow. Most of the races are around bush tracks which can vary according to the local terrain. The Victorian tracks are flat, tracks in New South Wales are hilly and the Queensland tracks are sandy. All races are conducted with specific rules and are run under independent race marshals.

BREED CLUBS AND SHOW DOGS
There are a number of main breed clubs in Australia. The SHC of New South Wales, The SHC of Victoria, The Siberian Husky and Alaskan Malamute Club of South Australia and The SHC of Queensland. However, there is no national breed club in Australia.

Siberian Husky registrations in 1986 were only 160 but, just 10 years later, 1,223 Siberians were registered. They are now in the top six in the popularity stakes. With the increasing popularity of the breed, there has been a corresponding increase in interest in showing. To obtain a Show Championship in Australia a dog must gain 100 points at Championship shows and win a Challenge Certificate. Each CC is worth 5 points, plus one point for each dog of the same sex beaten (including one point for the dog itself). A Best in Group award is worth 25 points. In January 1998, the Grand Champion title was introduced for those dogs gaining 1,000 points. Numerically the largest show is the Melbourne Royal Show. It has around 6,000 exhibits and is also the largest in the Southern Hemisphere. Each state has its 'Royal' show and these are usually the largest in the State, and the most publicised.

DENMARK
The first Siberian Husky was imported to Denmark in 1968. Allerellies Candy was owned by Grethe Westring. She came from Gunnar Allerellie in Canada and her first litter was born in March 1969. The sire of the litter was Baro, owned by Alf Andersen from Norway.

The following year, Candy gave birth to a pure white litter, all males. It was the first pure white litter in Europe. The sire was Green Beret's Snowy Arctic, imported from Holland from Nancy van Gelderen-Parker.

Grethe Westring, of Chukchi Kennels, imported a number of males who formed the foundation of the breed in Denmark: Green Beret's Snowy Arctic, Alaskan's Kaltag of Anadyr in 1971 from the Norrises' Anadyr Kennel in Alaska, Klondike's M'U Kaltag in 1977 from Switzerland, Kree Vanka Frosted Finnstar from Finland in 1976 from Stina Blomqvist and Chilkoot's Moody from Switzerland in 1981.

The breed is still relatively small in Denmark with around 175 members of the Danish Siberian Husky Club and about 25 Siberian kennels.

Elly and Jorgen Hansen started their kennel in 1970 and introduced Arnack of Tamarack in 1977 and Balou of

Bodil Nielsen (Setzoniaze). All the dogs in the team are descendants of Grethe Westring's dogs.

Sikusalingmiut in 1982. Balou sired a litter of six who were born in quarantine in England in 1984. The Hansens imported Bacon av Vargevass in 1996 from Karsten Gronas, Norway.

There are around 15 races a year held in Denmark. The majority of races, particularly in recent years, are held on dirt using three-wheeled rigs due to the lack of snow. This is a growing necessity for many who work their dogs.

The Danish Siberian Husky Club holds five shows a year and many of the show dogs also work. 1999 saw the 25th anniversary of the Club with Karsten Gronas judging the breed.

FINLAND

One of the very early mushers in Alaska was Finnish-born Johan Johannson (John 'Ironman' Johnson) who won the All Alaska Sweepstakes race in 1910 – a distance of 408 miles – in a record time of 74 hours, 14 minutes and 37 seconds.

While Ironman Johnson was involved with Huskies in Alaska in the very early stages of the sport, it took some time before the first Husky was imported to Finland. She was Anya-Alyeska and she arrived in 1965, brought from Switzerland by Kerstin Almi. The first litter in Finland was bred by Esa and Raili Mantysalo, who were also the first people in the country to start running sled dogs in harness. Winter temperatures in Finland can be below 40° Celsius and, since the country is quite sparsely populated, it is not too hard to find quiet roads, woods or lakes on which to run Huskies. Particularly in the north, it is possible to travel for days without seeing anyone. The only problem for mushers is that the traditional occupation for the locals is reindeer farming. Reindeer and Huskies do not always mix very well!

Esa was the first chairman of the Finnish Siberian Husky Club (FSHC) and he won many racing championships. His first Siberian was a bitch called Kanakanak's Kishka. Kishka came to Finland in whelp to Monadnock's Konyak of Kazan. She had six puppies: one female and five males.

One of these puppies, Ahtojaan Piko, was bought by Stina Blomqvist (Kree Vanka kennels). Most of the breeding behind Kree Vanka dogs is Anadyr (Earl and Natalie Norris, Alaska). Stina imported Green Beret's Snowy Angara who was successfully bred to Alaskan's Siber II of Anadyr and she kept two puppies. Stina showed and raced her

Siberians and her team won the Finnish Championship three times in a row.

In 1967 there were about ten Huskies in Finland – at the time the Finnish Siberian Husky Club was founded. Stina Blomqvist was a founder member.

The first sled dog camp took place from February 24th to 26th 1968 at Lokalahti. Eight club members, ten Siberian Huskies, two Alaskan Malamutes and three Samoyeds attended. Over the next few years the club's activities developed and more dogs were registered. Contact was made with the other Scandinavian countries and regular races were held with

Nugget of Calivali – one of the original imports from the USA who has had a significant input to Finnish pedigrees.

Norwegian and Swedish teams.

In the 1970s, the first Huskies in Finland were black and white, mostly with blue eyes, having come from American show lines. Discussions began about the different types of dog when the Norwegian dogs were beating the other teams by miles in the 1977 Championships. Could it be that their dogs being from working lines had something to do with their success? This was a turning point for the Siberian Husky in Finland.

Many active mushers started to rethink their teams and dogs were bought from many working lines in the USA, Norway, Canada and Holland. Most notable were Arctic Trail's Who of Kelson, Igloo Pak's Candy To, Nugget of Calivali, Alaskan's Victor of Anadyr, and Arctic Trail's Wing. Candy, Nugget, Victor and Wing were the foundation of the new lines in the breed. Although they all raced they were rarely shown because of judges' opinions towards the working Siberian. Many types can be found in Finland and some breeders continue to keep the original imported type. However, the club survives as a result of the active racing scene. The FSHC became the official breed organisation for the Siberian Husky registered with the Finnish Kennel Club. In 1975, 500 Huskies were registered, giving a total of 1,300 dogs, 500 members, 330 teams in races and 230 show attendances.

In the 1980s, about 300 dogs were registered each year. Mushing became

Polar Speed Tukkimo (Igloo Pak Candy To x Arctic Trail's Who of Kelso).

more and more popular. Many of the original people who started in the three-dog class in the 80s have become the top drivers of today. Some mushers have turned to the Alaskan Husky to achieve even faster times. The Alaskan Husky, often a Siberian Husky-cross, is considered to be a faster dog and more successful in racing, but many members of the FSHC welcomed the challenge to breed better and faster Siberians. The results are seen today. Reijo Jaaskelainen (Polar Speed kennel) and Erkki Rantanen (Endhill's kennel) have shown that their Siberians are still competitive sled dogs.

The FSHC has arranged special training for judges and encouraged them to attend events where Siberians can be seen in a more natural environment than the show ring: at races and working trials.

Knowledge of running dogs increased considerably during the 80s with many guest speakers coming from the USA to give seminars – people such as Dr Charles Belford, Natalie Norris, Vincent Buoniello, Harris Dunlap and later Doug Willett. The general feeling has been that the Finnish dogs are excellent: some even going so far as to say that the dogs could prove to be the salvation of the racing Siberian Husky.

Finland was declared as a rabies area in 1988 and as a result show and working dogs were unable to compete in Norway and Sweden although they could continue to travel to other parts of Europe.

Nowadays, the FSHC has many roles to play. It is the official racing representative for the Finnish Kennel Club. It has also obtained official status for a working test and a race test for the Siberian Husky. For many years the FSHC has gathered pedigrees and other information about Huskies in Finland. For anyone requiring general information on the breed, the FSHC has produced the *Blue Book* which is like a Bible for the Husky enthusiast. It contains a great deal of information, from the history of the breed to health and dietary matters.

Reijo Jaaskelainen is arguably the most important breeder in Finland. His Polar Speed Kennel has produced excellent sled dogs through the years. Originally he based his breeding on Doc Lombard's Igloo Pak, Calivali, and Lloyd Slocum's Arctic Trail dogs. Later he started to use mainly dogs from his own Alpirod team (the Alpirod was a major European race). Now the name Polar Speed is widely known and respected along with Reijo's excellent dog handling skills.

Other notable kennels are Hopevuoren and Goosak. Hopevuoren kennel was founded in 1978 with breeding based on some of the Vargevass dogs from Norway. The kennel includes several types but most of the dogs are long-distance racers.

Goosak kennels was founded in 1986. The dogs are mostly of Seppala strain from America, the foundation males being Satin of Sepp-Alta, Ash of Markovo and Tagil Barney. Satin is a son of Beowulf of Sepp-Alta, Doug Willett's lead dog in the early 80s. Ash of Markovo was an important stud dog in Karsten Gronas's Vargevass kennel.

RACING

The first race in Finland was held in 1969 with the number of races growing over the years. There are races of many types, from the 100-metre dash to long-distance races held over several days. One speciality in Finland is the Triathlon. This includes a sprint race, a sprint with extra load on the first day and a longer run on the second day. When the Alpirod came to an end there was no long-distance race in Europe, so the Scandreaen race was organised by John Elomaa. This race

Eila Kuusinen (Lumirinteen), still active in Finnish racing today.

covers a distance of 686km in six days with 38 teams from many different countries attending.

The Finnish Polar Speed team won the race, beating the Alaskan Huskies – very satisfying for enthusiasts of pure-bred Siberian Huskies. Other races that Reijo has done well in with his Siberians are the Nordic marathon and Finnmarkaloppet.

Every year the FSHC organises a special show just for Siberians. The judges are breed specialists and are familiar with working Siberian Huskies. Dogs must pass in order to get the title FIN MVA (Champion and an acceptable result in a typical race test).

There are two kinds of test: the race test, in which the dog must finish the race within a certain percentage of the time of the winner. The second test is a

handling test which must show that the dog can obey the common sled commands. The handling test is divided into two classes: lead dogs and others.

The title FIN KVA (Finnish working champion) requires the same kind of race test result, a more demanding handling test result and a good show result. These titles are granted by the Finnish Kennel Club, the sole official registration organisation in Finland.

OTHER ACTIVITIES
Several kennels have Siberians that compete in Obedience and Agility. Nadja av Vargevass (Leo av Vargevass-A ex Tatjna av Vargevass-A) owned by Tuija Valkama has taken part in both sports.

A few years ago some entrepreneurs did something that had never been done before in Finland. They moved North and started to use their dogs as they were originally intended, to help provide a living for their owners.

The beautiful countryside of Lapland and Eastern Finland provides perfect surroundings for holiday tours. These people arrange sledding tours with their dogs, giving tourists the opportunity to run their own team of dogs in Finland.

FRANCE
The 1960s saw the arrival of the first representatives of the breed on French soil, but it was not until 1972 that the first Siberian Huskies were registered with the French Kennel Club (Societé

Madame Stodkovic's May Be The Best De La Vallee de Morava: one of the top-winning Siberians in 1999.

Centrale Canine, or SCC). These were Kamut Kyat of Anadyr, Koliam du Patis au Roi, and Alaskan's Igloo of Anadyr. There was only one official breed club, and the Siberian Husky was included in the Réunion des Amateurs du Samoyede et Chiens Nordiques (later renamed the Club Français des Chiens Nordiques). However, the breed's popularity grew quite rapidly from the early 1980s and, in 1989, the breed club Siberian Husky France was founded. It is the official breed club in the country today. After a considerable boom in the number of registered puppies in the mid-1990s, when as many as 6,000 puppies a year were registered by the SCC, the registration rate has settled at between 1,000 and 1,300 annual registrations.

Early bloodlines present in France included dogs bred by the Alaskan Anadyr kennels, the Yeso Pac kennels, Monadnock kennels, and Karnovanda, as

well as imports from the Leich's Forstal
Kennels in England. Among the first
well-known French Siberian Husky
kennels were the Amarit Kennels (F.
Mannato), l'Aurore Boreal (E. Oudin),
O'Pieds Agiles (Y. Belmont), Amarok
(M. Paranthoen) and Pointe Barrow (M.
Heitzmann). Early French Champions
include such Siberians as Ch. Lupa (C.
Leneuf), Ch. Chamak (F. Mannato), and
later Ch. Amarok's Sergei (M.
Paranthoen). Today's well-known French
kennels include Baker Lake (E. Barba-
Lopez), la Baisse de Leveillat (C.
Bedarride), L'Igloo des Sables (G.
Denance), Reves de Neige (B. Abadie)
and Crystal Lake (M. Di Tommaso). One
of the top Siberians of the 1990s has
been French Champion, (Brevet level 2)
Eikinah de la Baisse de Leveillat (owner
M. Cayol). Also present in the show ring
are imports from Arctic Sun kennels
(M. Manco) in Belgium and Tundrafoot
kennels of Mr Knight in Canada.

French Siberian Husky breeders are
active on the international show scene,
and quite a number of French-bred
Siberians have won the coveted title of
FCI International Champion over the
years. In the spring of 1999, Baker Lake
kennels were particularly successful, with
four different Siberians winning at top
International shows. Ch. Moody Blues
of Baker Lake took the Best in Specialty
Show title and the Golden Cup for his
owner Miss Angelique Pasquier of
France, at the Hungarian Siberian Husky
Club National Specialty in May, under

Hungarian judge Peter Harsany. Two
weeks later, Ch. Mitka Temudjin of Baker
Lake, owned by Mr G. Bellac of
Switzerland, won both the title of
Mexican Champion and that of 1999
World Show Champion, at the FCI
World Dog Show in Mexico in May,
under judges Rafael de Santiago of
Portugal, Betsy Merill of Canada, and
Jean Fournier of the USA. At that same
show, Ch. Norma Jean of Baker Lake
(Marilyn) won the Mexican
Championship and was Reserve to the
1999 World Winner bitch. One week
later, Ch. Maybeline of Baker Lake was
awarded the CAC/CACIB by Dutch
judge Mrs Nancy van Gelderen-Parker,
at the 1999 French Championship
Show in Paris. This win allowed
Maybeline to finish her International
Championship title.

RACING
Racing began in France at the Col de la
Schulcht in 1979. Siberian Husky teams
driven by Yannick Belmont, Franco
Mannato, and Monique Heitzmann-Bene
were among the leading teams of the
period. In 1980, the first racing
organisation was founded, the Club de
Pulka et Traineau à Chiens. Racing
kennels include O'Pieds Agiles
(Belmont), Wolvescreek (S. Lescao), and
Blau Fontein (I. Travadon), as well as
several smaller kennels. The Anadyr
bloodlines are still prevalent in racing
teams, but the 1990s have seen imports
and breeding of stock such as Sepp-Alta

and Igloo Pak lines, the latter for the most part via the Polar Speed Kennel of Reijo Jaaskelainen. Other American racing stock has also been imported recently or used, with dogs from the Northome and Fortsalong Kennels behind a few racing lines.

The 1990s saw the arrival of leading Siberian drivers such as Dr Daniel Fournier and Dr Philippe Travadon in the unlimited and mid-distance classes; Sophia Lescao and Isabelle Travadon in unlimited; Claude Tomasino and Raymond Arnoldi in 8-dog; Thierry Fontaine and J.J. Court in 6-dog; Eric Guiral, Lionel Poncin and Gerard Chaudron in the 4-dog class;

The Polar Speed Kennel has produced a great number of top racing dogs. Pictured: Polar Speed Jasmini.

and Serge Heitz and Patrick Geley in the Scandinavian-style pulka and ski-joring classes.

The SCC issues a provisional pedigree to registered puppies, and to obtain a definitive pedigree and thus authorisation as breeding stock, dogs in France must be 'confirmed' by a specialist judge. The requirements are very strict for the Siberian, even down to the number of teeth and tail-carriage. Siberian Husky France organises a yearly National Specialty show. Here dogs are examined individually by breed judges and given a qualification ranging from Excellent to Insufficient. Then the jury vote on which of the Excellent dogs or bitches are of the quality required to earn the title of 'recommended' dog or bitch, with breeders also having the possibility of competing with breeding stock and their offspring for the title of 'élite'. The Recommended males and females are then ranked from 1st to 4th, with the first and second placing obtaining, respectively, the CAC and Reserve certificates, which count towards the title of French Champion.

The breed club and the SCC also offer a working title: the 'Brevet de Travail'. This title consists of four levels, from the simple 'Brevet' to the 'level 3 Brevet'. Dogs must compete in teams registered in specifically accredited races, and the teams must be within an allowed time relative to the average of the three top teams per class, in order to qualify for one of the Brevet levels. A dog that

Thierry Fontaine and his six-dog team, 1999.

receives the Brevet level 1 can compete in official working classes at shows, and this title is a minimum requirement to obtain the French Championship show title. Dogs that attain the Brevet level 3 (the highest level) can compete for the title of Working Champion.

Aside from showing or sledding, Siberians also participate in Agility competitions, and with the recent recognition of Obedience competition by the SCC, there should be a few determined Siberian owners trying their luck at obedience trials in the future.

GERMANY
The Siberian Husky has been in Germany for at least 30 years and is now a very popular breed. The first registered dog in 1967 came from Switzerland, Kamtschatka's Burning Daylight from Thomas Althaus, a well-known breed specialist and judge. The famous American Mulpus Brooks the Roadmaster was his grandfather. Other imports in the late 1960s came from Holland from Matanuska (Liz Urlus) and Green Beret kennels (Nancy van Gelderen-Parker). Some came from Denmark, from the late Grethe Westring's Chukchi kennel. Anneliese Braun-Witschel started her Alka-Shan kennel in November 1972 and is known for her excellent working/racing dogs.

Anneliese Braun-Witschel acquired her first Siberian in the early 70s, Kara of Chippoorwill, while training horses in the Eastern United States. Kara was a fine-boned piebald of show line background (Alakazan and Marlytuk dogs as well as a dog called Columbia's Admiral). Kara and her son Eskimo of Northland Husky went back to Germany with Anneliese.

Kara was bred to Matanuska's Chenuk Taku (Dutch lines based on Anadyr dogs). This breeding produced her 'A' litter, Alaska Lady of Alka-Shan and Arctic Melody of Alka-Shan. Lady was bred to half-brother Eskimo to produce what Anneliese calls her "first important team dog", Black Magic of Alka-Shan. In 1977, she bought Kamtschatka's Borax, a black male from H. Knott (European Champion many times after L. van Leuwen went out of the sport). Knott started off using Kamtschatka as his kennel affix but later found that it was used by T. Althaus of Switzerland so he

changed to Ketchikan, although his early litters could not have their names altered.

Borax came from half Canadian show stock and half Dutch (Anadyr). The Anadyr half included Voodoo of Anadyr and Green Beret's Snowy Dancer (Alaskan's Babiche of Anadyr ex Alaskan's Ginny), the latter a sister to Snowy Angara who was behind the early Scandinavian Siberians. Anneliese described Borax as having 'show' conformation: a smooth gait, intelligent, and one of the toughest dogs she has ever owned.

Elegance-Elecktra of Alka-Shan was Anneliese's foundation bitch who, when bred to Arctic Melody, produced Hideaway of Alka-Shan, her most famous leader and stud during the early 80s. Hideaway, when bred to his mother

Kamtschatka's Borax joined the Alka-Shan kennel in 1977.

Anneliese Braun-Witschel, pictured with Elektra and Hideaway in lead, with littermates behind in point – Happy and Enjoy; Black Magic running on his own, with B-Timber (behind in right wheel) and Kamtschatlea's Borax at left wheel.

Elegance-Elecktra, produced her N, R and Y litters whose progeny were the mainstays in Anneliese's Championship 8-dog team in 1985.

In the late 80s the Alka-Shan kennel introduced dogs from contemporary racing lines to cross with their dogs. One particular dog, Ely of Sepp-Alta, brought in the agouti colouring and was used at stud many times in Germany, the Netherlands and Belgium, and his influence was significant. Anneliese also used Hercules of Sepp-Alta (known as Hank) on her bitches. This produced eight members of her winning 10-dog team (distance racing) in the United States. Anneliese is still active in working and racing Siberians today.

There have been several other imports from Canada and Finland which go back to old New England lines.

Volker Schon imported Innisfree Ferg and Innisfree Savage Sam from America. These two can be found behind many show kennels in Germany today. Sam's father is the well-known Ch. Innisfree's Sierra Cinnar.

From 1969 to 1979, about 175 litters were registered and after the union of East and West Germany the gene pool has greatly increased. Today, there are around 15,000 registered Siberian Huskies with 700 Siberians being registered each year.

CLUBS IN GERMANY

The main kennel club in Germany is the Verband für das Deutsche Hundewesen (VDH) – a member of the Fédération Cynologique International (FCI). The members of the VDH are the breed clubs which are authorised to give special requirements for the breed, for example a certificate for controlling hip dysplasia. In Germany, the Siberian is judged to the AKC Standard.

There are two breed clubs for the Siberian Husky. The first club started in

169

1968, Deutsche Club für Nordische Hunde (DCNH). Today, this club looks after 24 different Northern breeds with the Siberian Husky representing the largest part of the club. The DCNH awards sled dog certificates to mushers. These are stated on the dog's registration papers. Their eyes must also be free from hereditary diseases.

The second club was founded in 1994 and called the Siberian Husky Club Deutschland e.v (SHC). There are around 250 members. This club is mainly for mushers who work their dogs in harness. For breeding purposes, a dog needs to obtain a working certificate. To qualify, the dog needs to have completed 100km on snow. This is not difficult as there are many races on each weekend during the winter months.

Innisfree Savage Sam, an American import, features in many German kennels.

Today in the show ring you may see some 30-50 Huskies being judged. These dogs are not only from Germany but from other countries such as Belgium, France and Italy.

The first sled dog race took place at Latrop (Sauerland) in February 1972 with three mushers from Holland. The next year there was an increase to 14 teams, at the first international sled dog race. This included four competitors from Germany.

Today there are around 800 mushers racing purebred Siberian Huskies and there are others who prefer to race Alaskan Huskies and other sled dogs. There are races for everybody and one can choose which to compete in.

ITALY

In 1975, Majo dele Tre Torri was probably the first registered Siberian Husky in Italy. She was a black and white bitch bought by Mr Modesto Contiero from an American living in Italy. This bitch became the first Italian and International Champion. In 1976, she was bred to Ch. Matanuska's Chenuk Taku. Mr Contiero kept a bitch called Yaska dei Navajos; she was the dam of Synuk dei Navajos who was used many times at stud.

The first import to Italy was in 1975. Monadnock's Happy Prince (Tawny Hill's Gaibryel ex Tawny Hill's Molina) brought in by Marisa Brivio Chellini, a well-known international show judge. At the same time Mrs Jessica Vallerino

Ch. Matanuska's Chenuk Taku (left), who was bred to the first registered Siberian in Italy, Majo dele Tre Torri (right).

imported a bitch from the UK called Forstal's Ivich (Forstal's Kassan ex Micnicroc's Nanuska), a litter sister to the first Champion in Great Britain, Ch. Forstal's Mikishar the Amarok.

However, dogs imported to Italy in the 80s had more influence on the breed and were the basis for future stock. Many were imported from Kathleen Kanzler's Innisfree kennel. In the late 80s, Maura Bensi imported Innisfree Golden Arrow, a red dog, and Star Enchantress, a grey bitch.

Many of the top winning Siberians of today are the children and grandchildren of the dogs from Mrs Bensi, Mr Contiero and Mr Cattaneo.

CLUBS
The Italian Nordic Breed Club (CIRN) was founded in 1976 to protect and improve some Nordic breeds.

The CIRN is an important and active club for Italian owners of Nordic breeds, breeders and judges. Membership has increased considerably, and the club has about twenty Nordic breeds including Siberians. The Siberian Husky is one of four breeds which have become very popular in the last few years, so the CIRN divided this group into four separate sections. Each section has its own representative and they organise shows, choose judges, plan seminars, and publish books on their breed. In 1998, the CIRN introduced compulsory checking for hereditary eye diseases and hip dysplasia, one of the first clubs to implement control of hereditary diseases.

*Italian and Swiss Champion Akzal
(Innisfree's Red Calypso x Yukon Shadow).*

THE SPORT
There are several working organisations which arrange races either on a regional or national basis. The best-known organisation is the Italian Sled Dog Club (CIS) which is under the FISTC and allows only purebred dogs at their races.

There is also the Italian Mushers Association (AIM) which allows all types of dog. The CIS organises the Italian Sled Dog Championship. In 1999, there were four races in the Alps in January and February. The teams are divided into seven categories. The best team from each category will participate in the Italian National and then go on to the World Sprint Championship.

There is also a middle and long-distance Championship which was held at Annaberg (Austria) in 1999. Finally there is a European Sprint Champion-ship held in Baqueira (Spain). In 1998, the Italian mushers achieved excellent results with Giovanni Nardelli winning the six-dog class (B1 category) and Alex Zanier winning the six-dog (B2 category) class at the International Championship.

THE NETHERLANDS
The Dutch Kennel Club year books for 1934 and 1939 contain pictures of a Husky. However the origins of these dogs are unknown.

It was many years before a Siberian Husky was registered – probably due to World War II. Liesbeth Urlus, an airline stewardess, first imported Siberians in 1966 from the USA.

They were Kayak Thunder Taku, a male, and a female, Vaskresenya's Tanana Taku. Liesbeth started breeding under the kennel name Matanuska but although she had a number of litters her influence on future stock in the Netherlands was not that great. Matanuska's Chenuk Taku was the sire of the first litter in Italy. He also sired Anneliese Braun-Witschel's 'A' litter when he was bred to Kara of Chippoorwill. He is behind many of the Alka-Shan dogs of today.

Els and Lau van Leeuwen (Kolyma) imported a number of dogs from the Anadyr Kennels of Earl and Natalie Norris. Alaskans Chatka of Anadyr, a silver-grey bitch, and a red and white male, Alaskans Sha-Luk-King of Anadyr, came to Holland shortly after Liesbeth Urlus's two dogs.

As Earl and Natalie both raced and showed their dogs, the Dutch breeders felt privileged to have good foundation stock. Other well-known kennels from the early days were Nancy van Gelderen-Parker (Green Beret, '69), Leo Van Groenewegen (Naoyaks, '70), Leo van Pieterson (Ilaranaitok, '73), Hyls and Nies Heeringa (Komaksiut, '75), Piet Van Nimwegen (Sikusalingmiut, '76) and others.

In the early 1980s, Doug Willett (Sepp-Alta Kennel USA) visited many places in Europe and wrote articles for the *Racing Siberian Husky* magazine, about many of the dogs he had seen in these countries. After this, Siberians from Holland had a huge impact in Western Europe and Scandinavia.

Nancy van Gelderen-Parker's Green Beret kennels was one of the first in the Netherlands. Pictured: Green Beret's Snowy Babbet, 1974.

The Siberian Husky Club of Holland (SHKN) was founded on 29th November 1969 and all the Siberian Husky owners of the time were present. The founder members of the committee were Liesbeth Urlus, Els and Lau van Leeuwen, Leo and Gerri Groenewegen and Nancy van Gelderen-Parker.

The main goal of the new club was to be united in maintaining a Standard-fitting working dog. One of the first rules was to X-ray for hip dysplasia.

The club started with 56 members and some 120 Siberians were registered with the Dutch Kennel Club. A club magazine is produced to keep members up to date.

The first club show was held on 7th March 1971, with 29 dogs. Today this show is often judged by foreign breed specialists. In 1998, the show had an entry of 125 dogs for breed specialist Karsten Gronas from Norway and Mrs Helga Vent from Germany. The dog Anartjok's Toesca (pictured overleaf) a lovely grey/white with brown eyes, aged six, bred by Karin van Eyk and owned by Paul and Maya Brunner was best dog and went BOB. The bitch CC went to Patouche of Novaja Semlja owned and shown by Ton Kievits.

The first race was held in Switzerland by the Swiss Club for Nordic Breeds in Axalp in 1966. Lau and Els van Leeuwen, and Leo and Gerri Groenewegen competed.

Until 1996 it was against Dutch law to run dogs in harness, so many people worked and raced their dogs in other

Anartjok's Toesca, Best of Breed and Best in Show, at the Siberian Husky Club of Holland Open Show, 1998.

countries. Once it became obvious how much these dogs loved their work, the law was changed and people are free to run their dogs.

NORWAY

The first Siberian Husky arrived in Norway in 1957, a dog called Pogo brought from Alaska by Gisle Bang. This dog was approved and registered as a Siberian Husky by the Norwegian Kennel Club. In 1958, Leonard Seppala gave the well-known Norwegian explorer and writer Helga Ingstad a white AKC registered bitch as a present. Her name was Molinka of Bow-Lake, and she had two litters with Pogo. The Ingstad family later imported Sepp and Sindy from Norvik kennel in the USA. They took the kennel name Brattalid, and this is Europe's oldest Siberian kennel. During

the 60s and the 70s came a number of imports to Brattalid kennel, their stock being based entirely on Anadyr lines.

Norway is good for winter sports and a lot of people enjoy outdoor life, so the increasing interest in Siberian Huskies was not surprising. The Norwegian Siberian Husky Club was formed in 1972. In the beginning, most people used their Siberians to pull pulkas or Nordic-sleds with a skier following, but among members of the club the interest in the sport of sled-dog racing began to form. This sport became very popular and a lot of races were held during the 70s. More imports arrived, some more influential in breeding than others. Up to 1981, about 50 dogs had been imported to Norway. Since then, a limited number of dogs have arrived. Norway has strict quarantine laws, which makes it quite expensive to import dogs. Today, there is still a four-month quarantine period from countries outside Europe, but since 1994, European dogs can enter providing they have been vaccinated against rabies and blood-tested. Norwegian mushers compete abroad and foreigners race here.

The most important changes came when the Swede Ingvar De Forest, Snowtrail kennel, made a trip to USA and Canada, and bought 11 dogs (three from Zero kennels, three from Igloo Pak, one from Arctic Trail, and four Anadyr dogs). With him was Karsten Gronas, of Vargevass Kennels, who bought two males.

Some of the imports from 1978 are key dogs in Norwegian and Swedish Siberian pedigrees today. The most important in Norway were the two Vargevass imports: Arctic Trail Fang and Yeso Pac's el Diablo. From the Swedish-owned dogs, the most influential were Zero's Dargo, Zero's Cider, Zero's Milky Way, Alaskans Mona of Anadyr, Arctic Trail's Amber, Igloo Pak's Beaver, Igloo Pak's Chena and Igloo Pak's Shagtoolik.

There have been some major debates in the Siberian world over the years, the main one, as ever, being show dogs versus racing dogs. There were a number of show lines in Scandinavia in the 70s, but with the growing interest in racing, they have never become very popular. Then the discussion moved on to Nordic racing. Race rules required a fairly heavy weight to be pulled in the pulka races, and the Nordic competitors bred for very large Siberians in order to be competitive with their dogs. Finally the weights were reduced and, as more people moved into sled-dog racing, the problem died out.

Finally came a major debate with the arrival of the Zero imports. Were they Siberians or not? This debate continued until 1985, when racing was opened to all dogs, purebred or not. Most Zero line breeders moved into Alaskan Huskies, and the debate cooled. Today a few kennels have chosen to have no Zeros in their pedigrees, a few still breed with mostly Zero lines, but most dogs in Norway are a mixture of most lines. Influential Zero imports in Norway,

beside the Swedish dogs, were Zero Bumper, Sparkey, Gleemer, Spaceman, Blizzard, Ruh-Hoe and Jeeree.

The highest numbers of Siberians born in Norway was in 1984, when 565 dogs were registered. Sled-dog racing had reached a peak just before the races were opened. Since then, the number has gradually reduced and has stabilised at approximately 150 dogs registered a year. The last American imports were Ash of Markovo, imported by Karsten Gronas, and Ezra of Sepp-Alta imported by Oivind Nord. Ash has been quite influential in Scandinavian breeding, Ezra to a lesser extent.

The most influential Norwegian kennel is Vargevass. Karsten Gronas obtained his first Siberian in 1965 and has stayed with the breed ever since. Besides the American imports, Thalitta of Kolyma was another influential dog in the early breeding. Karsten has always had one of Norway's largest Siberian kennels and has been a leading racer. He has exported many dogs over the years. Having raced in open sprint classes, he has more recently switched to mid-distance racing.

Other important dogs in Norwegian pedigrees were bred by well-known open class racers, like Asbjorn Erdal Aase, Kjetil Hillestad (Speedos kennel) and Roger Legård (Teamster kennel).

Another person who imported a number of dogs which have influenced Scandinavian breeding was Christen R. Andersen (Finnemarkas kennel). He imported Natomahs Neka Nemik and

Lisa, Arctic Trail's Graatass, Igloo Pak's Daisy, Zero's Sparkey, Gleemer and Ruh-Hoe.

Another kennel that has exported a number of dogs and is influential in many recent Norwegian kennels is Vargteam (Ole Dag Lovold).

The interest in racing purebred dogs has substantially reduced in Norway since the races were opened. People who were interested in competitive racing went into Alaskans and gundogs, people interested in recreational mushing chose purebred Nordic dogs. Norway has so much wilderness and many people own a Siberian team and enjoy mushing without ever setting foot at a race. In the last few years, the interest in distance mushing with Siberians has increased and new kennels are getting started, but interest in sprint racing with Siberians is non-existent. In Sweden, there are a number of competitive sprint racers.

In both Norway and Sweden the interest in showing Siberians has been very low. However a new interest in show dogs is emerging and some imports have arrived in both countries.

SPAIN
The first Siberian was imported by Bartolome Bernal in 1981. Verite's Magic Maiden, a female, became a Spanish Champion. In 1983, a male followed – Kohoukek's Jaro Jaro. Jaro became an International Spanish Champion and was the father of other Spanish Champions such as Donna De la Espanola, Zorba de la Espanola and Jaro de la Espanola. In 1984 a female, Kortar's Tara of Madrid, was imported from the US and was the dam of Isla de la Espanola who was Best of Breed at the National Specialty in 1989. Sekene's Image of Innisfree, a Canadian Champion, was imported to Spain by Bartolome Bernal and became the Reserve dog at the World Show in 1987. Innisfree Chateaugay was a top producer in the 80s and can be found in many pedigrees today.

Fernando Salas started his kennel, Lupiak, in 1982. His first Siberian came from France, Ch. Tarnak and in 1984 he won the National Specialty.

Arctic Blue is the kennel name of Rhonda Hayward which started in 1983. Rhonda imported a female from the US, Portbay's Lady Foxfire, the dam of Arctic Blue's Winter Melody who finished her Championship in 1991. Ch. Arctic Blue James Bond, a black and white male, finished his Championship in 1991. He is a son of Innisfree Chateaugay and Karnovanda's Shasta Groznyi and won the Spanish Kennel Club's National Specialty in 1993.

Ch. Artic Blue's Texas Ranger, a red and white male owned by Antonio Llado Gaspar and Daniela Vidal Leaver of Winterfrost kennels, was bought as a puppy in 1994 and became World Champion in Austria in 1996, then a Spanish Champion and also went on to BOB at the National Specialty in 1998.